The Parent's Guide to Exam Stress

The Parent's Guide to Exam Stress

YEAR 7 TO GCSEs, A LEVELs & MORE

Practical, positive ways to support and motivate your child

Katharine Radice

GREEN TREE
LONDON • OXFORD • NEW YORK • NEW DELHI • SYDNEY

GREEN TREE
Bloomsbury Publishing Plc
50 Bedford Square, London, WC1B 3DP, UK
Bloomsbury Publishing Ireland Limited,
29 Earlsfort Terrace, Dublin 2, D02 AY28, Ireland

BLOOMSBURY, GREEN TREE and the Green Tree logo are
trademarks of Bloomsbury Publishing Plc

First published in Great Britain 2026
Copyright © Katharine Radice, 2026

Katharine Radice has asserted her right under the Copyright,
Designs and Patents Act, 1988, to be identified as Author of this work

For legal purposes the Acknowledgements on p. 246
constitute an extension of this copyright page

All rights reserved. No part of this publication may be: i) reproduced or transmitted in any form, electronic or mechanical, including photocopying, recording or by means of any information storage or retrieval system without prior permission in writing from the publishers; or ii) used or reproduced in any way for the training, development or operation of artificial intelligence (AI) technologies, including generative AI technologies. The rights holders expressly reserve this publication from the text and data mining exception as per Article 4(3) of the Digital Single Market Directive (EU) 2019/790

Bloomsbury Publishing Plc does not have any control over, or responsibility for, any third-party websites referred to or in this book. All internet addresses given in this book were correct at the time of going to press. The author and publisher regret any inconvenience caused if addresses have changed or sites have ceased to exist, but can accept no responsibility for any such changes

Disclaimer: The material contained in this book is for informational purposes only. No material in this publication is intended to be a substitute for professional medical advice, diagnosis or treatment. Always seek the advice of your GP or other qualified health care professional with any questions you may have regarding a medical condition, including mental health concerns, or treatment and before undertaking a new healthcare regime, and never disregard professional medical advice or delay in seeking it because of something you have read in this

If you need further guidance on relaxation techniques, deep-breathing exercises, or other ways to help your child with the physical and psychological consequences of stress, there is advice available on the NHS website. If you have concerns about your child's wellbeing, it is best to reach out for professional advice at an early stage

A catalogue record for this book is available from the British Library
Library of Congress Cataloguing-in-Publication data has been applied for

ISBN: PB: 978-1-3994-2527-8; ePUB: 978-1-3994-2526-1; ePDF: 978-13994-2529-2

2 4 6 8 10 9 7 5 3 1

Typeset in IBM Plex Serif by Lumina Datamatics Ltd
Printed and bound in Great Britain by Clays Ltd, Elcograf S.p.A.

To find out more about our authors and books visit www.bloomsbury.com and sign up for our newsletters
For product safety related questions contact productsafety@bloomsbury.com

for my parents

A NOTE ON LABELS

- **KS3** refers to Key Stage 3, i.e. Years 7–9
- **KS4** refers to Key Stage 4, i.e. Years 10–11
- **KS5** refers to Key Stage 5, i.e. Years 12–13

A NOTE ON SCOPE

This book focuses on how adults can help young people who are at secondary school. I've used the words 'parent' and 'child' throughout, but it's a book designed for any adult who is keen to support a young person in their care.

For most of life's day-to-day experiences children look to the everyday people in their lives for support. There are times, however, when a child's needs go beyond what a parent, carer, relative or friend can provide. **If you think your child is experiencing stress or anxiety at a level that needs professional medical or psychotherapeutic help, please do not hold back from reaching out for this help at an early stage.** It is much better to seek professional advice before stress or anxiety has developed to an extent that is harder to treat. See further guidance on p182.

Contents

Introduction ... 8

Part 1 – Groundwork: Thinking about the context for exam stress ... 23

  1: Understanding the causes of pressure and stress ... 24
  2: Differences in perspective between adults and teenagers ... 42
  3: Understanding what school is like today ... 57

Part 2 – How to help your child: Key techniques ... 71

  4: Creating constructive conversations about school ... 72
  5: Establishing effective work habits ... 93
  6: Building a balanced perspective ... 111

Part 3 – Age-specific advice ... 127

  7: Getting started at secondary school ... 128
  8: Tests and exams in Years 7–9; choosing GCSE subjects ... 148
  9: Creating positive expectations and a constructive work rhythm in Year 10 ... 168
  10: Revising effectively for GCSEs; tutoring ... 187
  11: Starting sixth form ... 207
  12: Getting ready to leave school ... 226

Acknowledgements ... 246
Bibliography ... 247
Index ... 250

Introduction

I don't want to talk about it

you don't understand

leave me alone

*why can't you just **go away***

I've been teaching in secondary schools and working with families for over 20 years but I can still remember something a parent said to me in my first year of teaching at my very first parents' evening: *my child doesn't tell me much about school.* I remember this because I've heard the same thing again and again in every parents' evening since then.

It's really hard to know how to help if you don't understand what's going on. Unfortunately for the parent-child dynamic, as children get older, they often find it harder and harder to open up to their parents. This is especially true if they're unhappy. Secondary school is a remarkable developmental stage: it's full of newness, challenge, excitement and opportunity, but your child's experience of it will inevitably be intertwined with the uncertain, vulnerable feelings of adolescence. There are bound to be moments when any and every child fears they're not good enough. Exams often crystallise these feelings: the results show who's doing *better* and who's doing *worse* and by exactly how much.

This is why I'm focusing on exam stress. Exams aren't the only thing that's difficult or important about secondary school, but they are central to the school experience and they'll probably define your child's perception of whether they're doing well enough or not. Throughout this book, I'll be giving you ways to make it easier for your child to talk to you about school and I'll be explaining how you can use these conversations to help your child develop a healthy, positive relationship with exams.

> **Student:** *My GCSE time was so bad. I lost so much weight that the doctor thought I was anorexic. If anything I was trying to put weight on, but when I get anxious my appetite goes. I got so overwhelmed and stressed. I was so locked into thinking only about exams it was like life wasn't happening.*
>
> **Do you find this quote surprising?** Many parents underestimate how stressful exams can be: I've regularly heard students in exam classes say something similar to the student above. In this book I'll be helping you see how to reduce the risk of problematically high stress levels.

How likely is my child to be affected by exam stress?

Problematic levels of exam stress are really, really common in schools today. When I was interviewing teachers and mental health professionals for this book, I asked them to put a number on it: *how many pupils did they think were problematically affected by exam stress?* The number varied – the more academically selective the environment, the higher the estimate – but the lowest estimate anyone gave me was 10%. At its highest, it was over a third. *Problematically affected* did not necessarily mean that the student was experiencing anxiety as a medically diagnosed condition, but it did mean that the levels of worry about exam performance were impacting physical or mental well-being.

> **Senior Leader (Pastoral):** *We're a large comprehensive. Exam stress is high on the priority list for me – it's close to the top – maybe even overtaking concerns about drugs, friendship, self-image. So much of the stuff I get sent is about anxiety / mental health and the research I read suggests that the reason kids are less happy is down to exam pressure.*

What can I do as a parent?

Supporting teenagers through exams can be difficult. As parents, we have to watch our children go through it; inevitably we're involved but – at the same time – exams are a school thing. We can see the fallout at home but the solutions often seem to lie elsewhere. Parents can end up feeling like spectators, watching the process but unsure how to help. Stress about exams can lead to frayed family dynamics where parents are worried, teenagers don't want to talk about it, and everyone wishes that there was a quicker, less gruelling route through.

This book will help you reduce the risk that exam stress builds to a problematic level and it'll help you maintain a positive family dynamic along the way. On p17 you'll find an overview, which will help you see at a glance where to find the material you're looking for. Before we get started, though, there are three things about exam stress that I need to introduce briefly first:

1. Exam stress makes it harder to do well
2. Common – and incorrect – assumptions about exam stress
3. Headlines about our role as parents.

Exam stress makes it harder to do well

Exam stress usually makes it harder to do well. I've put that in bold because lots of people find a bit of pressure quite motivating and – as a result – lots of parents think that they need to keep telling their children to *take school seriously because exams really matter.*

I'd agree with the principle – teenagers should take school seriously and exams do matter – but whether this is the most useful thing for a teenager to hear regularly at home isn't quite so clear-cut. Today's teenagers are already under significant pressure on multiple fronts: as a parent, there's a risk that you end up increasing this pressure in a way that is counterproductive. Drive the pressure up too high and your child will end up sitting their exams in the midst of the multiple negative consequences of high levels of stress: racing heartbeat, nausea, sleepless nights, muscle tension, brain freeze, catastrophisation, panic attacks. The list of possible consequences goes on.

> **Y12 Student:** *It feels like everything is going fast – like the exams are coming – it's faster and faster. It makes it harder to work – it makes me panic – my brain just goes blank.*

Common assumptions about exam stress

When I'm working with parents, I regularly encounter incorrect assumptions about exam stress. I'm headlining some of the most common assumptions here so that we can deal with them right away.

The first one is this: ***if a student's getting good grades, they've got nothing to worry about.*** No one enjoys the prospect of a test if they think they're going to do badly, but that doesn't mean there'll be no stress at all if your child is on track to do well. It's not just a fear of failure that drives high levels of exam stress; there's also the fear of disappointment, regret or self-blame if – unexpectedly – the results aren't as the student hoped. The likelihood of this disappointment materialising might be miniscule, but this doesn't necessarily stop the fear.

Some of the teenagers who feel most anxious about exams are the ones who are most invested: they're working the hardest, they're on track for success and everyone is telling them that *they'll be fine*. But they may feel worried all the same because if it doesn't go as well as everyone expects, the cost will be significant. There'll be the shock of the surprise, the feelings of disappointment and – above all – the sense that those hours and hours of input were in some way ill-judged because things didn't pan out as planned.

It's worth remembering that the more a child cares, the higher the stakes. The fear of failure is inextricably bound up with the wish to succeed. It's simply not possible to have one without the other. As parents, we need to think carefully about what our children feel is on the line in their exams and not assume that if the grades are looking fine, the pressure must be OK.

> **Student:** *People saying 'You don't need an A*' doesn't help either: yes, I don't need it, but I want it, and wanting it makes me feel scared.*

The second incorrect assumption goes like this: ***if my child's doing no work, they're clearly not stressed***. Often, this isn't true either. Two of the most common consequences of high levels of exam stress are procrastination and disengagement. If your child doesn't want to pick up a pen, it's entirely possible that this is because the balance has tipped over and they don't feel confident that their efforts will generate the right return.

> **Early Career Teacher:** *On the face of it, the exam stress looked just like she wasn't putting the effort in.*

There's a similar misunderstanding at the other end of the motivation scale: ***if my child's working really hard, then everything's fine***. Probably, *yes* – but not always. As you read this book, you'll hear me refer to hyperengagement. This typically appears when students believe they can do it but fear that it might go wrong. These students turn to overworking as the antidote, believing that if they just keep on churning out past papers, working for longer, reducing their breaks, trying to concentrate harder, they'll be more on track to success. In its early stages, hyper-engagement looks like the winning ticket: the student is hardworking, conscientious, committed. Over time, however, hyper-engagement can warp into a damaging perfectionism, exhausting the student and reducing their capacity to think calmly in the context of difficult material.

> **Student:** *At first, it felt good to be good at schoolwork. I was top of the class in most of my classes. This made me feel good, but there was always a sense of unrest – if I got 39/40, then I felt that I should get 40/40. I'd always focus on the mistakes. I was always doing more work than other people and it got to the point where it became unhealthy. Now I find myself obsessing about everything I do – if it's not perfect then it's terrible. It's like a constant weight on my shoulders, always the sense that it could be better, it could be better.*

The final incorrect assumption happens when parents are trying to work out how to help: ***when I was at school, what I did was...*** It's entirely natural to try to understand your child's experience of school by thinking back to your own experience of exams but – as I'll be exploring further in Part 1 – your memory of your school days and your child's experience are two different things. Thinking back to what you did can end up distorting the picture, bringing in assumptions that don't apply to your child and distracting attention away from finding out and thinking about what your child needs.

Headlines about our role as parents

Exam stress can build to problematic levels because it often has multiple causes. If your child is already experiencing high levels of stress, there will be a range of external factors that are probably fairly obvious, such as how positive they feel about school in general, the difficulty of the subject content, the future competitiveness of the job market, the challenge of getting places for training programmes or university courses. The easy visibility of these factors can lead to the assumption that they are the only factors in the mix.

This means that sometimes we don't pause to think about what else is contributing, too, especially when those other factors are much harder to see. As parents, sometimes the most difficult material to think about is the causal role that we might – unintentionally – be playing. This is especially true if your main aim is to help your child be healthy, happy and do well at school. It can be difficult to think about the ways in which well-intentioned actions can have unintended, negative consequences. This is why I'll be starting Part 1 with chapters that focus on bringing invisible factors into view.

If you'd asked me five years ago if my own children were going to experience potentially problematic levels of exam stress, I'd have blithely and naively said *probably not*. I'd been teaching for years: I understood the world of schools and I reckoned I had a well-informed, balanced, healthy relationship with the whole process of taking exams. I assumed that the exam years wouldn't throw up any surprises. I was wrong.

My naivety had two dimensions: first, I knew my own perspective on exams but I hadn't paused for long enough to try to imagine why my children's perspective might be different. Second, I assumed that just because I didn't *want* my children to feel too much pressure, they'd find a zen-like equilibrium in their schoolwork, gliding along in the sweet spot of working hard enough but without problematic levels of stress. I assumed that we'd magically end up in a situation where they'd feel the same way as I did about exams.

When the exam years hit, I was shocked by the pressure my children felt. This made me realise that I needed to think searchingly about the differences between my perspective as a parent and my children's experience as teenagers. I also realised that I needed to think searchingly about the external factors in my children's experiences *and* about my own role in the pressure they were under. I'll be discussing all of this in more detail as this book progresses, but there are two things it's worth pausing on briefly now.

1. Pressures on teenagers today

This is a book about exam stress, not smartphones, but social media is even more central to the adolescent experience than the process of sitting exams at school. This wasn't the case for our generation: this means that we need to rethink how to help our children so that it's calibrated to the world as it is for them, today, with all its notifications, ratings and judgement.

There's been plenty of attention given to the impact of social media on confidence and self-esteem – Jonathan Haidt's bestselling book *The Anxious Generation* offers a thought-provoking discussion of this. Collectively, we are facing serious questions about whether young adolescents should even have access to smartphones, social media apps and so forth. The focus on self-esteem, however, means that we're at risk of ignoring the digital world's impact on time.

For the stressed-out teenager, the interactions on social media may or may not be a positive experience, but there's a guaranteed impact on time and mental bandwidth either way. Keeping up with the ever-unfolding notification stream means that teenagers are much, much busier than before, even if it doesn't look like they are doing very much when they are lying on their bed, scrolling away. There is an obvious cost from this to the emotional and mental energy they have left to engage with schoolwork.

All this means that pressure may exist in ways that we, as parents, may not have expected and our initial assumptions about how much capacity our children have to shoulder the inevitable pressure of exams may not be correct.

> **Assistant Head, Teaching & Learning:** *Pressure at home, pressure at school, difficult exam expectations – I think it's probably a perfect storm of these things.*

> **11–18 SENDCO:** *I'd say this to teachers and parents: put yourselves in the teenager's chair for 10 minutes: how would you feel if that was you?*

2. The balancing-act as a parent

Parenting decisions often centre around this question: *Do I lean in and get involved, or do I stand back and let them get on with it?*

The tipping point between under- and over-involvement as a parent is an important consideration: do too little, and the child isn't supported; do too much and the child doesn't have enough space to grow through developing their own independence. One of the biggest challenges in the parent-child relationship is that this tipping point keeps shifting: it's quite clear that a baby needs their parent to do everything for them and that an independent adult should be free from the apron-strings, but as for the years in between...? It's a difficult call. Parenting teenagers is often a murky landscape of trying to work out whose opinion should prevail – yours or your child's?

How hard should you push your own children? This is a difficult question: throughout this book, I'll be offering frameworks to help you answer it. It's particularly difficult, though, when parents are worried that their children aren't working hard enough. The instinct is often to lean in, push a bit harder, do what you can to avoid the risk that your child gets lower grades than they should.

The question of how hard to push crops up whenever I do a workshop for parents on exam stress. When I highlight the very real need for parents to help reduce the pressure that some students feel, someone always raises their hand and asks something along the lines of *but if I back off as a parent, what happens if my child underachieves*?

I wouldn't be surprised if you find yourself asking the same question as you read this book. This is because many of the suggested conversation sequences later in the book prioritise creating the space for your child to make meaningful decisions for themselves, supported by their parents' interest, but not curtailed by values and expectations that belong to their parents, not them. There will be many places where it may feel that I'm suggesting that you *back off and listen* rather than intervene and direct from the outset.

But if I back off, they'll do nothing at all! If this is your worry, you are not alone. I've heard the same worry from many parents over the years. There are two things that are worth holding on to here: the first is that I'm suggesting that you *listen to your child's viewpoint first* and this isn't the same thing as backing off altogether. *Listening first* means making sure you've understood a situation well enough to find a set of expectations that are deliverable; it's a route to avoiding a battleground situation where child and parent are so misaligned in perspectives that conversations exacerbate conflict rather than provide an opportunity to connect and support.

The second thing to remember is that it's worth running the counterfactuals. If you know that your interventions are creating conflict, then, whatever the grade outcome, the conflict is a given. The counterfactuals, therefore, are threefold: Version #1 is that the status quo continues and your child gets the grades you are hoping for; maybe these are worth the damage the conflict did to your relationship but maybe they're not. Version #2 is that the grades don't materialise and all you are left with is the fallout from the conflict. Version #3 is where you prioritise imaginative and meaningful dialogue so that you can help – rather than argue with – your child. The evaluation is this: in which version is there more guaranteed gain?

How to use this book

This book is divided into three sections.

- **Part 1 – Groundwork: Thinking about the context for exam stress.** In Part 1, I'll be focusing on the range of factors that feed into the pressure that teenagers feel, offering ways for you to think through the impact you have as a parent and the type of support your child might need as they move through secondary school. Doing this groundwork will help you understand better how to use the techniques introduced in Part 2.

- **Part 2 – How to help your child: Key techniques**. In these chapters, I'll set out three key areas where you can support your child: creating constructive conversations, establishing effective work habits and building a balanced way of thinking. These techniques will help you support your child, whatever age and stage they are at.
- **Part 3 – Age-specific advice**. In Part 3, I'll explain how the educational context changes as your child gets older. In these chapters, you'll find more granular guidance about how to support your child as they progress through secondary school.

Each chapter is a mixture of explanation and guidance. If you want to jump straight to the ideas about how you can help, look out for the icons in the margin.

☆ In Part 1, you'll see this star icon next to the sections that outline what you can do to understand your own context better.

★ In Part 2 and Part 3, you'll see this star icon next to the material that shows you how you can help.

There's no one way to read this book: you may find it useful to read it as a linear sequence, one page at a time, or you might prefer to flick through to the material that connects most directly with your context. The groundwork in Part 1 will help you understand the context of exam stress better, but you don't have to start with this: you might prefer to start with Part 2 or Part 3 and return to the groundwork later if you're looking for a deeper understanding. Where material in one chapter builds upon material earlier in the book, I've included references to pages you might like to refer back to.

I'd ask you, though, to remember this caveat: a book like this is inevitably general in nature but each family has their own, individual dynamic. This is why you'll find boxes with questions throughout each chapter which create the space to think about how the material I've included relates to your family. The questions focus on extracts from interviews with teenagers, (either at school or looking back on their experiences), teachers and mental health professionals from a broad range of contexts. Each interview extract conveys one person's experience or thoughts, but I've only included material that resonated with things I've heard many times over in schools, at conferences, and when I've been running workshops for parents on exam stress. It is, of course, up to you what you do with the questions: I hope you'll find them helpful as a springboard for reflection, but there's no harm in skipping the questions that don't pull you in.

Please read this book with a healthy dose of scepticism: some material may suit your context, some material may not. If you're intrigued but unsure about whether something I've suggested would work for you, it's probably worth discussing it with your teenager. As you'll hear throughout this book, taking an interest in your child's views about what helps and what doesn't is a core part of the advice. After all, there's no one who knows more about their experience than they do.

What if my child is neurodivergent?

Each child has their own needs but – within a classroom – the needs of each individual child tend to overlap. In a mainstream classroom, the fundamental needs – such as clear instructions, a supportive atmosphere, plenty of repetition, an accessible framework for progress – apply to everyone; it's the degree of need that varies. The general nature of the advice in this book means that it's targeted at these core needs and so it's likely to be relevant – to some degree – to all children who attend a mainstream school.

If your child has special educational needs, the strategy sheets that your school's SEND and Inclusion team have created will help you identify the material in this book that is most appropriate for your child and they'll provide a steer for how to adapt it. So, for example, if you know that your child needs stepped instructions, dealing with just one thing at a time, then this will mean that some of the suggested conversation sequences will need to be broken down and taken gradually. If you know that your child's needs make school more exhausting for them, then this should inform the balance between work and rest that is right for your child, and so on.

The higher the level of special educational needs, the more you'll need to adapt this book's general advice. It may be worth reaching out to your child's SEND or Inclusion lead: they know your child and will be able to help with this. But I hope that the general nature of this book will still offer something of value because it will help you understand the world of mainstream school better. The better you understand the environment your child is within, the better you'll be able to support them in navigating their route through.

Realistic expectations

As you read this book, you'll find that the importance of realistic expectations is a recurring theme. When I first became a parent, my own expectations of what parenting would be like were entirely unrealistic. I had no idea how difficult it would be. I've often felt a gut-scrunching lurch when I've realised that the consequences of something I'd done were not as I'd intended. Ironically enough, it's a whole lot easier to write a book about parenting than it is to actually be there on the ground, working out what to do next.

The parent-child relationship is a difficult one because it has to keep changing as children grow up. We have to keep recalibrating around the unpredictably evolving landscape of our children's development; this becomes harder during adolescence because teenagers often find it hard to understand their own feelings and reactions. It can take time to think through complex issues like identity, values, expectations, responsibility and uncertainty: all of these ingredients are there in the exam mix. Sometimes it takes time to strip away assumptions which belong to ourselves, not our children. Sometimes we're so focused on trying to help teenagers *become* someone that we don't pause to see them as they are. I've come to realise that all this makes it inevitable that there are missteps and moments where we need to adapt.

So, if there are moments where you too feel the lurch of wondering if you need to do something differently, I'd encourage you to see it as a good thing, even if it's uncomfortable. You'll find that these are the moments where something shifts and it becomes easier to see how to help. And after all, we're parents: that's all we're trying to do.

PART 1

Groundwork: Thinking about the context for exam stress

> Part 1 focuses on understanding the factors that contribute to exam stress. It's designed to create the space to think about the impact you can have as a parent and the type of support your child might need in the context of school as it is today.
>
> Part 1 lays the groundwork for the practical guidance that will follow in Part 2 and Part 3, but this doesn't mean that you have to start with Part 1. You may prefer to get straight to the detail of how you can help: you'll find this in Part 2 and Part 3. If you do this, it may be helpful to return to Part 1 at the end, so that you can build a deeper understanding of how to adapt the advice to your own context.

CHAPTER 1

Understanding the causes of pressure and stress

Student: *It's hard to be faced with that thing of having to disappoint people.*

When I was interviewing students for this book, I often asked them what they felt stressed about in the context of exams. *Disappointment* came up again and again in their answers. Many of them said that it wasn't the grade itself that they feared, it was the disappointment that might accompany that grade. Some students told me that they feared disappointing their families or teachers; some students said they feared their own disappointment if grades arrived which somehow weren't what they'd been hoping for.

What counts as disappointing? I've seen students burst into tears at an A grade and whoop with delight at a C. Disappointment is relative; it's calibrated to expectations. This is why I'm starting Part 1 by focusing on the factors that shape a child's beliefs about the grades they feel they *should* be getting and the degree to which they feel that they're doing *well enough*.

Central to this chapter will be the idea that there's always a risk of disappointment on results day and the vast majority of teenagers will know someone who's done *better* than they have. *Not the most upbeat opening to a book*, you might be thinking. I'd agree – and if you're looking for positive, practical guidance about how to help your child do well, I promise there's plenty of this coming up. But we're starting with the less cheerful side because exam stress centres around the prospect of things going wrong. My opening question, therefore, is this: what sets the benchmark for *my grades are OK* and how would your child feel if they weren't?

> **Education and Safeguarding Consultant:** *I think there's the aspect of environment: what happens if you are not performing as highly as others in your class or what happens if what you're doing doesn't meet your parents' expectations?*
>
> What expectations do you have for how your child will – or should – do?
> What expectations does your child have for how they will – or should – do?
> Why do these expectations exist?

Carrying the uncertainty: Will my grades be OK?

In our examination system, students prepare for months and years for something that – coursework excepted – is graded entirely on how it goes on the day. Surprises happen all the time: no student knows for sure in advance what their grade will be. It doesn't matter how hard someone works or how many past papers they rack up: there might be very good grounds to believe a particular grade is the most likely outcome, but – emotionally – there's a country-mile difference between *looks very likely* and *you'll definitely be fine*.

> **Y13 Student:** *There is no certainty. This is the scary thing. The certainty that adults have – saying, 'Oh you'll be fine'. This doesn't match up to how I feel – I'm not certain, even if the teacher is.*
>
> How certain / uncertain does your child feel about their likely exam results?
> How do they respond to this feeling?

UNDERSTANDING THE CAUSES OF PRESSURE AND STRESS | 25

This uncertainty is gruelling: it's a major contributing factor to the exhaustion that many students feel in the long run-up to exams. The longer the exams are in view, the longer the period where your child will be thinking about whether or not they'll get the grades that they want.

Uncertainty is exhausting for anyone – take, for example, the *do I think about it/do I try not to think about it* wait for news from a job interview – but it's particularly difficult for adolescents. Adolescence is a developmental stage that is full of uncertainty anyway: teenagers don't know where they'll land at the end of it. They don't know who they'll become, they don't know whether they'll be able to create an adult life in the way that they hope, they don't know how valuable or lovable they'll be to others.

In this context, exam grades can feel uncomfortably definitive. They create a label: they form part of the written-down, external identity that a student carries with them through school and then onwards into the workplace. The grades are only part of a teenager's identity, for sure, but they are one of the most clearly quantified, permanent, universally understood, inherently comparative and competitive labels available during the teenage years.

Throughout this chapter, therefore, I'll keep returning to the following idea: how much of your child's sense of self is wrapped up with the need to get a particular set of grades? How fixed are they in their beliefs about how their future is supposed to look? How confident do they feel that they'll continue to be loved and valued, even if the grades *could have been better*? And – most importantly – are they clear about the value of other parts of their identity which don't get labelled as routinely and visibly as their progress in Maths?

> **Student:** *You're constantly questioning, 'Am I good enough, will this be OK?' You don't get that answer until results day and that's a long time afterwards.*
>
> - What if the grades aren't OK? What would your child do next? What would you do next?
> - What would help your child find a positive route through, even if there are surprises on results day?

Who am I supposed to be? Key factors

Did you ever – as a teenager – have to do the fairly excruciating task of describing your personality? Perhaps as a PSHE task or similar, or for a self-portrait in English or as a foreign language exercise? I use the word *excruciating* because – for teenagers – it usually is. Self-definition is difficult for a teenager, not least because there's often some tension between honest self-knowledge and the preconceived ideas about who you're *supposed* to be.

When teenagers begin the long run-up to exams, they arrive on the start line with a set of expectations already in place about the person they're supposed to be and – accordingly – the grades they're supposed to be getting. If we're going to understand exam stress, therefore, we'll need to think about the factors that shape these expectations. Let's discuss the four key factors now.

Factor #1: How adults describe a child

It's worth noticing that a child's sense of who they are begins with the way they are described by others. As adults, we label children all the time. *She's the quiet one. He's always in trouble. They just love reading. You're so good at dancing, aren't you!* To some extent, this is inevitable. Like so many parenting habits, its roots lie in early interactions. Small children can't talk and so we talk about them and we talk for them: *I'm sure they'd love a slice of cake. Alex! It's time for cake – you'd like a slice, wouldn't you?*

As a child grows up, they become more self-aware. Their emerging personality doesn't always follow a smooth, predictable route plan: sometimes there's a friction between their own sense of self and the person their families assumed they were or expected them to be. This friction can be like sandpaper, creating painful, slow-to-heal grazes.

Some of the descriptions adults give to small children are trivial – *they're really into Paw Patrol* – because they relate to interests that are easy to give up. *No I'm not, Mum! Paw Patrol is for babies.* This sort of label is temporary – it can be thrown off easily when it no longer fits – there's no sandpaper-like friction when it no longer applies. But what about the labels that are harder to remove?

Some of these labels are positive: they relate to things that the parent may want to stay true. *She's always wanted to be a lawyer*. Is it straightforward for the child if they think that this aspiration is no longer desirable or fulfillable? Is it comfortable for them to say, *actually, I'm not sure I can be a lawyer; I don't know what I want to do, but I don't think it's that*. Would that sort of statement be greeted with the same sort of cheerful smile and applause as, for example, *I think I'm ready to clear out all my Lego* – would we view it as progress or not?

Some of the labels are negative. *The problem is that you're lazy. You never take school seriously enough*. The parent may want to let go of these labels, but the more the child hears them, the more they stick. Making changes to attitude usually happens incrementally: how easy is it for a child to believe that the initial, small steps of progress will be worth it? Or will the effort feel pointless because the child fears it'll be invisible, easily drowned out by the all too familiar idea that they *haven't worked hard enough again*?

Factor #2: Copying others at school

A child's sense of the person they're supposed to be isn't only impacted by what others say about them. Most children would feel pressure to be a certain way even if no one had ever labelled them or voiced a particular expectation at all.

Evolutionary behavioural theory looks in part at the instinctive pulls that shape human development. As a species, we are designed to learn from each other. An essential component within this is the ability to select – at a fairly instinctive, unthought-about level – who it is that we learn from and what it is that we copy. Peter J. Richerson and Robert Boyd's book *Not by Genes Alone* describes two different categories of the impulse to emulate others:

- **Conformist bias:** this refers to the pressure we feel to copy what the majority are doing.
- **Prestige bias:** this means that we instinctively aim to copy role models who are prestigious within our communities and who are praised or admired by others.

Conformist bias is particularly acute during adolescence: as teenagers prepare to separate from their parents, fitting into other social groups becomes doubly important. Conformist bias casts a pressure even if it's never verbalised. I can still remember a form-time session on peer pressure in my first year at secondary school. The resources suggested to us that we'd all be tempted to smoke or take drugs because one of our friends would be telling us to or criticising us when we didn't. A couple of years down the track, I found myself surprised at how inaccurate this picture of peer pressure was: when all my friends started to smoke, I felt pressure to join them even though none of them ever said anything directly to me that suggested they cared whether I did or I didn't. The pressure existed simply because the majority were doing it.

Conformist bias plays a significant part in exam stress. Conformist bias means that your child's relationship with exams will be shaped partly by what is standard in their school. If most of your child's friends don't seem to care about schoolwork, you'll need to think harder about how to help your child find the motivation to go against the grain (see further, Chapter 5). Conversely, if your child is at a school with a reputation for good grades and which is packed full of teenagers from families who care about good grades, *caring about good grades* will permeate the daily atmosphere of the place, adding to your child's general feeling that exam results really do matter, whether or not they are hearing the same message at home.

> **Y12 Student:** *When I see other people who are very stressed, it makes me more stressed – I think 'Why aren't I more stressed about the thing they're freaking out about?'*
>
> Can you think of situations where your child has been worried about something because of the way someone else is responding to it?

Prestige bias creates a pressure that is more explicit because it arises from the way other people react to something. Which students get celebrated by your child's school? Who goes up to collect prizes during assembly? Who appears in the newsletter? What does that implicitly signal to your child every day about the type of person who is considered valuable to others?

Factor #3: Copying others at home; sibling rivalry

Conformist bias and prestige bias play out at home just as much as at school. It's entirely natural for a child to want to match the grades that other people in their family got. In addition, children are usually acutely aware of what their parents find impressive in other people. When a child overhears their parent saying to a neighbour, *your granddaughter got straight As? That's amazing! How brilliant! Well done – you must all be so proud*, it's prestige bias which means the child may feel pressure to do the same, even if their parent is separately telling them that *we don't mind what you get*.

> **Y11 Student:** *Some people are anxious because they think they should be getting better grades than they are, maybe because other people in their family have got certain grades.*
>
> Is this relevant to your context? Does your child feel pressure to live up to other people's achievements in your family?

The instinctive impulse to replicate other people's success can be especially strong between siblings. Children are often very different from each other, but this doesn't mean that they don't feel the need to match each other's achievements. In addition, sometimes parents refer to one child as a way to motivate another child to change their habits.

> **Student:** *Comparisons aren't helpful. My brother and I work differently – he kept being compared to me, but he gets it done a different way.*

> If you have more than one child, do they feel that they need to get the same grades as their sibling(s) or are they at ease with the idea that their approach and outcomes might be different? (See further, p36.)

Factor #4: Praise

Praise is the mechanism through which we express whether or not someone is fulfilling our expectations of who they should be. When I was interviewing students about exam stress, a recurring theme was the idea of the burden of praise. *Burden of praise* might seem like a strange concept: we tend to think that praise is always a good thing. Receiving meaningful praise makes children happy, yes, but this doesn't mean that praise is entirely without complications.

It's a good thing when parents praise their children, but it's worth checking in with what you praise them for: each allocation of praise tells a child that *this part of who you are is valuable – it's pleasing to others; if you keep being this way, we'll probably keep praising you.* Inevitably, this means that it embeds a risk factor: *What happens if I stop being this thing? What happens to the praise then? What happens to my value and self-worth?*

> **Y13 Student:** *It's about meeting an expected standard. If you don't meet that standard, there'll be disappointment. In my own mindset I have certain standards I set for myself – I want to prove myself to myself. If you're not meeting that standard then you feel disappointed in yourself. You can't separate your own disappointment from the fear that you might disappoint others.*
>
> If your child is highly motivated, what is the *expected standard* that they're trying to meet? Have they told you? Have you asked them?

☆ **How do you talk to / about your child?**
The questions below will help you think through what gets praised. They will also help you think about how this defines your child's identity or self-worth, and how secure that self-worth may feel for your child. Does the praise relate to aspects of your child's life that they can control, such as their attitudes or reactions to events? Or does it relate to aspects they have far less control over, such as test scores, approval from others, or future life outcomes? Does the praise implicitly suggest that they need to be the same person they were before, or does it create flexible space for them to change as they get older?

- **What gets celebrated or rewarded?** Do you offer treats for good school reports or a family celebration if a test score goes well? Does your praise focus on outcomes or attitude?
- **What gets criticised?** Is it something that your child could do something about or is it something they had no control over, such as how other people in their class did in a test?
- **How do you talk about your children to others?** Do you encourage your child to tell other adults about their school results, sports trophies, music certificates or extracurricular achievements, implicitly suggesting that the value of these activities is encapsulated by the degree of success? Or do you talk about everyday things that are not tied up with external judgement from others, such as their interests and the things they've been doing *without* reference to certificates, prizes and so on?
- **Do you expect your child's interests to continue**, suggesting perhaps that it'd be such a shame to give something up because they've been *doing so well* at it? Or do you encourage your child to be interested in how they are changing and developing as a person, asking them if they still enjoy something in the way they used to or whether they've become interested in something different?

> **Y13 Student:** *The stress levels can get exacerbated when there's been a lot of praise in the past – this is definitely something I've experienced, It can get a bit stressful when you've done well and people expect you to continue with achieving at that level.*
>
> What would happen if it looked like your child was doing less well than they did in the previous school year? How do you think you would react?
> What would you use as your metric for this? Would it be their marks in school assessments?

The need for a flexible attitude about outcomes

I'm going to repeat one of the starting points for this chapter: your child won't know for sure what their grade outcomes will be until those grades arrive. Tolerating this uncertainty is much harder if a child believes that their grades *have* to be a certain way.

If your child has a particular dream, that's great: it'll give them a focus and something to work towards. I'm not for one second suggesting that they should water this down by assuming that all results, grades or careers are much of a muchness. Aspiration is important and it needs to be cultivated. But I am going to suggest that it's worth thinking about how straightforward it is for your child to handle the prospect that their grades or future career might turn out to be different from the one that they're hoping for or that they feel is expected by others.

All children benefit from a flexible approach to their futures, but – perhaps counter-intuitively – it's particularly important if your child is still quite young. As I'll be discussing in more detail on p39, the spread of marks within one and the same year group widens as children get older, sometimes in surprising ways. Take a Y6 class: the proportion of children who might seem to be on track for high grades at GCSE will be much larger than the number of children who will actually be on track by the time they get to Y11. As a parent, caution is needed: if a young child is excited by the prospect of an impressive career, it's entirely healthy to nurture this ambition but only if there's space for things to change over time if they need to.

> **Boarding School Housemaster:** *I've had kids in tears saying that their mum will be embarrassed by what they get. Often this is the kid extrapolating from what the parents say – they've been told what to get to meet an aspiration and they interpret this as 'I'll be an embarrassment or a disappointment if I don't'.*
>
> - Does your child think that you want their future to pan out in a particular way?
> - Have you asked them what they think your expectations are? Is their perception correct?

Responding to future career plans

As adults, we're bizarrely interested in getting children to pin down their future life plans. *What do you want to be when you grow up?* This is a go-to conversation starter, no doubt because it creates a friendly point of connection between the child and the adult world. The problem is, though, that we respond in different ways to different plans. If a child tells their parent that they really want to be a brain surgeon, it's easy for the parent to be enthusiastic about this aspiration. If a child says that they're up for joining an organised crime ring, I'd hope that most parents wouldn't start saying *that sounds great*.

Every moment of excitement about a possible future pathway, however, creates the beginnings of an expectation about that pathway. Excitement is a good thing, but the key question is this: is the excitement balanced by flexibility? If a child is interested in becoming a brain surgeon, is it still open to them to become excited about something else? If you've always hoped that your child will go to a certain university, is it straightforward to celebrate grades which fall short of this?

> **Senior Leader (Pastoral):** *We also see direct pressure from parents to kids: I was in a meeting with a student who is predicted a B at A level; they're working really well and I was telling them how impressed I was with their attitude, but their parent turned round and said, 'But they need an A to get into university'.*
>
> Do you think that your child *needs* a particular grade?
> If you do, how will that shape your child's feelings about the grades they are supposed to be getting?

☆ Thinking through how you talk about your child's future

The questions below offer the chance to think about whether or not your child's future already has clear labels and expectations. The questions also provide the chance to think about the margin of tolerance for what counts as *being OK*. If the hoped-for grades don't arrive, how straightforward would it be for your child to gather up their resilience, see past this temporary disappointment and crack on constructively with something else?

- When your child was younger, did they say what they wanted to be when they grew up? Do they still want this career? If they still want it now, are they aware that they might change their mind as they grow and develop?
- When you talk to your child about possible future careers, do you encourage them to keep several in mind?
- If your child has decided they're really keen to get a place at a particular sixth form or post-school course, how did you react? Did your response confirm their belief that this option is much better than others? Or did your reaction celebrate their aspirations *and* encourage them to be interested in the benefits of the alternatives too?
- Does it worry you if your child doesn't seem to have a long-term plan already decided? Or do you encourage your child to keep an open mind about decisions until they're closer and easier to make?

I need to be clear, though: in encouraging flexibility, I'm not suggesting that aspiration reduces. The key point is this: **too much stress makes it harder to succeed and too rigid an aspiration increases the stress levels**. If you want your child to work effectively, unhampered by problematic levels of stress, they'll need to be motivated, aspirational *and* they need to be able to tolerate the risk that – no matter how hard they study – their grades might not work out.

> **Y13 Student:** *Whatever happens, it's not the end of the world – this helps. It helps to know you'll still have a job at the end of the day, that your life won't be over.*
>
> - What would happen if your child didn't get the grades that they're hoping for?
> - What would help your child believe that disappointment hurts, but it's possible to move through it into something positive?

☆ Dealing with differences

On p33, I said that achievement levels spread out more widely as children get older, sometimes in surprising ways. This is why a flexible attitude about outcomes is needed, but there's another consequence: as children get older, secondary school exam grades make the differences between students much more visible. In Y7, a group of friends might think that their relationship with school is broadly similar; by Y11, the differences between them will be much more obvious. This can increase the pressure that your child feels to replicate someone else's achievements.

This might motivate your child to work harder, but it might leave them demoralised and – as Chapter 5 will discuss – feeling demoralised is one of the main reasons students disengage and stop trying. As a parent, you may need to help your child deal with these emerging differences so that they can learn to be clear about – and confident in – their own strengths. Let's explore this further now.

If your child is unhappy or problematically stressed because they feel they're not as good as they should be, or not as good as someone else in their class or their family, broadly speaking there are three different ways to respond:

- **Route #1** tries to mitigate the stress by denying the difference, perhaps by telling the child that *they're just as good* as whoever it is, or by saying the point of difference *really doesn't matter*.
- **Route #2** tries to close down the difference by telling the child that they can meet their expectations if they *put in more effort*.
- **Route #3** focuses on building a nuanced, flexible, more balanced understanding of outcomes and differences.

There are obvious downsides to **Route #1**: it can feel to the child like you're fobbing them off with reassurance that ignores the reality of the difference, or that you're suggesting that their feelings aren't really valid. It's a response that ends up closing the conversation down rather than opening it up, reducing the opportunities available to you to support your child effectively.

Route #2 can be supportive and motivational, but it can also have its problems. It's not always possible to close down the differences and – as Chapter 5 will discuss in more detail – if you want to motivate your child to work more constructively, giving a fairly vague suggestion to *put in more effort* isn't always the answer. Children tend to need something much more specific and attainable than an undefined suggestion to *try a bit harder*.

Route #3 offers something different. It is centred around taking an interest in the child's perspective and helping them understand why it's natural to feel the way that they do. *I understand why it hurts sometimes to see your sister getting higher grades* – this offers more consolation than the suggestion that *there's no need to be upset*. Understanding and recognising why differences can be painful makes it possible for a child to access the empathy that they need to recharge emotionally (see further, Chapter 4 and Chapter 8).

But empathy isn't the only thing you can offer: you can also help your child learn to see that the hierarchy within one sphere shouldn't be generalised to a hierarchy overall. A higher grade in Maths is just that: it's only about Maths. It doesn't mean that the Maths-whizz is better in every regard.

Does that sound so obvious that it's scarcely worth saying? As later chapters will discuss, however, it's not necessarily obvious to a child. Younger children think in fairly generalised ways (see further, Chapter 6): if you're told at primary school that you're the *star of the week*, it's natural for a child to equate good work at school with being the best *person* overall. At secondary school, children are old enough to realise that winning a prize for Maths is about Maths, not their whole self, but so much attention is given to exam grades that it can be hard not to feel that success in the exam sphere is much more important than anything else.

☆ Recognising value elsewhere

The sting in the public exam system is that the expectations are designed *not* to be fulfillable for everyone. Take a look at the GCSE outcomes on www.gov.uk: with the exception of the Covid years, the pass rate at GCSE sticks at approximately 66%. This means that, on average, for any individual GCSE, roughly a third of all students fail the exam. Move up through the grades and the percentages decrease: the A grade equivalent of level 7 and above is just under 20%. If you're looking for top grades, in 2024 only 1,270 students in the entire country got straight 9s.

At school, your child will hear day in, day out about the exam expectations that they're supposed to fulfil. Teachers have to do this: it's their job. The question for you as a parent is this: at home, do you want your messaging to be similarly dominated by the need to be what the examiner wants you to be? It's a good thing when teenagers take exams seriously, but do you really want your child to feel – by default – that being good at exams is *more* important than being good at anything else?

I ask this question because a meaningful, constructive route through life isn't all about exam grades: it's about finding your strengths and capitalising on these. You – as the parent – see your child in the round; you have the opportunity to take an interest in any and every one of their strengths, whether or not there's a GCSE or A level attached to it.

As you turn the pages of this book, you'll find plenty of advice about how to support your child in preparing for exams, but you'll also find advice about how to help your child remember that exams are not the only measure of value. If your child comes home crestfallen because someone else is *doing better in English*, do you really want the only solution to be getting better at English? Or do you want to help them work effectively so they can give themselves the best chance for their English exam *and* – at the same time – help them remember that there are multiple routes through life, multiple strengths, characteristics and dispositions that matter, and that although exam grades get a huge amount of airtime, they only represent one part of a person?

What happens when marks go down, not up?

On p33, I said that achievement levels spread out more widely as children get older. This is partly because public exams are designed to separate children into widely spread categories; that's their function for the job market. But the spread in levels of achievement is also because schoolwork gets harder. For most students, this means that marks are likely to go down, not up. 10/10 is possible in a short, primary school spelling test; it's unlikely to be possible in the same way for a much more subjective and sophisticated sixth form essay. This means that the final type of pressure we need to look at is the impact of the changing school context and what happens when a child feels that they are doing less well than the previous year.

If your child finds school difficult, there's likely to be an increasing need for you, as their parent, to provide a counterbalance to the exam experience as they get older. Counterbalancing doesn't mean saying that school doesn't matter: there's nothing constructive at all about undercutting what schools are trying to achieve. Counterbalancing means helping your child remember the other things that matter as well. If you make sure your child has things in their life that they know they are good at, this will help prevent feelings of *not doing well enough* at school spreading out into much more damaging, pressurising feelings of failure more generally. What's more, if your child is clear about where their strengths lie, this will create confidence they can draw on elsewhere: this will help them do better in the areas they find more difficult.

The increasingly demanding context of the school environment can also impact the child who gets high grades. Supportive parenting often means helping your child realise that finding something challenging doesn't necessarily mean that they're *no longer doing well enough* or that they're at fault in some way just because they're not getting the same marks they got the previous year.

I remember asking an A level pupil at the end of Y13 what she thought she'd learned most about success. She was a top-grade student in all areas and had a place at Oxford. *I've finally learned that 70% is just a number*, she said, *it's not a marker of my worth. It sounds so trivial and obvious when I say it now, but at GCSE I always got high 90s. I put so much pressure on myself to maintain these scores. I understand now that I have to interpret my progress relative to the difficulty of what I'm doing.*

I've been focusing so far on the expectations which are attached to your child's grade outcomes, but these aren't the only type of expectations in the mix.

As parents, our experience of our own time at school creates another set of expectations about what our children should – or should not – be doing. Teenagers often feel that their parents don't understand their point of view, and so the next chapter in Part 1's groundwork focuses on this: what are the likely differences in perspective between you and your child and how can you bridge these so that you can understand how to support your child effectively?

KEY IDEAS

- Your child's feelings about their exam grades will be shaped by their beliefs about the grades they are *supposed* to be getting.
- Expectations are shaped by what adults say and by what others are doing: teenagers have an instinctive impulse to conform to what the majority are doing or to copy what gets praised in others.
- Children change as they get older, sometimes in surprising ways: keeping an open, flexible perspective about future outcomes will help reduce the stress children feel and it will make it easier for your child to stay motivated.
- You can support your child by thinking about what gets praised and by encouraging them to keep an open mind about the future.
- Exams test a limited range of things; you can help your child build their sense of self-worth if you encourage them to notice and value parts of their character / skill set that aren't tested by exams.
- Schoolwork gets harder as children get older; marks are more likely to go down than up. You can support your child by helping them build a realistic understanding of their context and providing a counterbalance if needed; the age-specific advice in Part 3 will help you do this.

CHAPTER 2

Differences in perspective between adults and teenagers

Student: *Parents try to relate back to what exams were like for them; they give advice but not with accurate information.*

Does your child believe that you understand what school is like for them? Do *you* believe that you understand what school is like for your child? Are you and your child on the same page about how much school should matter?

In this chapter, I'll be exploring the potential gaps between your view of school and your child's experience; understanding these gaps will make it easier to see where you need to listen imaginatively to your child in order to empathise with and support them. I'll also be encouraging you to think about ways in which your perspective or values may be different from your child's. Being aware of these differences will make it much easier to have meaningful and constructive conversations that will help your child approach exams in an engaged and motivated way (see further, Chapter 4).

Do you understand what school is like now?

I'm not the first teacher in my family – far from it. My mother was a teacher, so was my aunt; I've got teachers in the ranks of my grandparents and great-grandparents. This meant that I grew up as a child listening to conversations about teaching all the time. *The thing is*, I used to hear, *that everyone thinks they know about education just because they've been to school themselves.* There's a lot of truth in this. The challenge for parent-child conversations about school is that education has changed dramatically in the last 20 years, even if the buildings and the labels we use to talk about education are roughly the same.

Your experience of school and your child's experience of school are two separate things. This section focuses on the way that, as parents, our own assumptions can distort the picture. Distortions can arise because the mechanics of cognition work in a way that often creates inaccuracies in understanding. I'm going to explain why this is, but I'm conscious that the next section will be very theoretical. If you're keen to understand more about how the human brain processes information, I hope you'll find it useful and interesting, but you may prefer to jump straight to the practical questions on p47. These are designed to help you take stock of what school was like in your day; this will then help you see more clearly which bits of your child's experience are likely to be different.

> **Y12 Student:** *I feel like parents don't understand – their exams were so long ago. It was different when they sat exams.*
>
> Did your parents understand your experience of school?
> Which parts of your teenage life seemed invisible to your parents?

How the brain processes information

If you haven't already read it, Daniel Kahneman's *Thinking, Fast and Slow* is a mind-blowing insight into how our brains work. It's a summary of his Nobel Prize-winning research into human cognition and – in particular – the distortions that are embedded into the structure of how we think.

His work divides the way we think and react into two broad categories. The vast majority of our thinking and reacting is done in a way which is quick and seemingly automatic: if I ask you what 2+2 is, the answer will have been in your mind before you even read the word *answer*. If someone takes a swipe at your face, you'll flinch. You had no immediate control over this thought process or reaction: your brain produced it pretty much instantly.

Kahneman's research focused on how this type of quick brain processing is different from the slow, deliberate, intentional thinking that we use if we're trying to work out something tricky. If I ask you what 3687 x 978 is, I'd be surprised if the answer popped into your head in the same way. Instead, you'll be aware that you've got a choice about whether to pick up pen and paper and think through to the answer.

Kahneman's research explored the mechanisms that our quick thinking and reacting uses. One of these mechanisms is the way that our quick-response cognitive processes make use of categories in order to understand new experiences. Categories allow us to quickly decode what is happening, but they also mean that sometimes we assume we understand something better than we do.

Using categories: The role of associative memory

The engine room behind the way we use categories to understand things is a process called associative memory: if you show me a picture of a church I've never seen before, associative memory will allow me to identify it as a church by joining the dots between details in the picture and similar features in churches that I've seen before.

As Kahneman explains, the key characteristic of our quick-thinking processes is that they are quick. This means that categorisation and associative memory work best with fairly blunt, unnuanced concepts:

it's much quicker and easier to lump things together as basically the same than to pause and be interested in the details that make them different.

Let's imagine I'm asking a friend what they ate on holiday. If they tell me the name of a dish I don't recognise, I might ask further questions about what it was like, but if they tell me they had a pizza, the chances are I won't ask for more details. Pizza is a category my brain recognises; associative memory allows me to process this information by equating it to pizzas I've already experienced. It's easy for me to feel like I've understood what my friend has told me, even if the pizza they ate on holiday bore very little resemblance to the pizza I pulled out of the freezer last week. Unless I deliberately remember to engage the slower, chosen thought processes which are interested in difference and nuance, the base level of brain processing won't pause to consider how untrue my previous concept of pizza might be in this individual instance.

How associative memory impacts the way we understand what our children tell us about school

Like many parents, when Covid hit and remote school started, I felt like I'd stepped into the matrix. One of my sons was 10 at the time. He was at a school where creativity was a central part of the ethos. He used to come home at the end of term with fistfuls of poems and creative writing. *How splendid,* I used to think, *how free and soulful! All this poetry – that's tremendous!* When *write-a-poem-about-a-tree* got set as a remote learning task, it was quite a shock: a free opportunity for self-expression it was not. Instead, it was a boot-camp-like process of following instructions on a worksheet. *Think of an adjective to describe the trunk; think of a colour to describe the leaves; write a three-word phrase that describes what it's like to touch the tree. Now use these words to complete this grid.*

I don't mean this to sound critical of the school's approach to creative writing: the upside to the worksheet was that it made it very straightforward to produce a poem and the kids were spared staring at a blank piece of paper with writer's block. But it does demonstrate that previously, the perception that I had – without thinking much about it – of my son's poetry writing was a long way away from what he was actually experiencing.

All this means that for conversations about school, there's a high risk of a gap between what the child says and what the parent understands. The language your child uses to tell you about school makes use of categories that your brain already understands; the challenge is that the associations of what the words *exam, test, revision* mean to you may be very different from what they mean to your child and in ways which – if we don't pause to ask and find out more about – we would never realise.

Uncovering your assumptions about school

If we want to remove the filter of interpreting our children's words through remembering our own experiences, the first step is to pause and notice what this filter looks like. No doubt you'll have memories that spring easily to mind when someone mentions the word *school*, but it's a slightly different thing to pause and think about what sorts of cognitive flavour hangs around words like *test, exam, revision, grades, getting a job*.

☆ Questions to help you identify your assumptions

The questions below offer a way to do a quick stock-check of your own associations and assumptions about key parts of the exam experience. After you've done this, it will be easier to notice where your child's experiences may be different from yours.

The list of questions is quite long: please feel free to move through it quickly. I've structured it into sections so that the different strands of the exam experience are clear, but your answers don't need to be detailed. Gathering up the headlines of what the questions immediately bring to mind will be enough to help you see more clearly the range of ways in which schools have changed. On p48 you'll find a short summary of what schools are like now so that you can compare this with your own school days; Chapter 3 will then describe the world of today's secondary schools in more detail.

Tests
- What was the first really significant test that you remember? Did you sit an entrance exam for secondary school? What was the preparation like for this? Did you do practice papers for months in advance or did you just turn up, do it and see what happened? Did you feel in advance like it was going to be difficult or easy to succeed? Were the stakes high?
- What sorts of tests did you do at secondary school? How frequent were they? How did you prepare for them? Did they feel like isolated events or explicitly connected to a long-term process that would impact your future?
- How did you feel before you took a test? What shaped your response when you got your marks back? Why do you think you responded this way?

Preparing for tests or exams
- Did mark schemes exist when you were at school? If you were preparing for a Biology exam, did your revision focus on learning labels, diagrams and so on, or did you also have to learn how to satisfy very specific mark scheme requirements?
- Did you have access to past papers? What practice materials did you have to help you prepare? Did you have revision guides? Were your revision resources boundaried and limited or did you have multiple options and a seemingly unlimited range of materials?

The importance of doing well
- Who cared about your school grades? You? The teachers? Parents? Siblings? Friends? What did other people do or say that impacted how you felt about the grades that you got?
- Did you worry about getting a job or did the future seem far off and unthought about?

Formal exams
- What age were you when you sat formal, public exams such as GCSEs or similar? What age were you when you first started to think about sitting these exams?
- Did your teachers refer to the exams repeatedly from an early stage, or was comparatively little said about them until the end?

Time
- How long did a year feel like when you were at school? When, for example, you were in Y10, can you remember thinking about the end of Y11 or was it too far away to be much in view?
- How busy were you at school? How busy were you when you came home from school? How much time did you spend with your friends? Did you have out-of-school extracurricular activities? Who decided how you spent your time – you or your parents?

Future choices
- When did you first start to think about career choices? Did you have career advice at school?
- When did you start to think about university choices or what you would do when you left school?
- As a teenager, how difficult did you think it would be to get a job as an adult? Or did you scarcely think about it at all?

School today: The headlines

In Chapter 3 I'll explore in more detail what schools are like now, but it's worth pausing here for some headlines. Children are formally assessed for SATs in primary schools and some children also sit high-stakes entrance exams for secondary school. For some children, these entrance exams involve months – if not years – of tutoring.

When children start secondary school, GCSEs are in the ether from the outset and firmly in view from Y9 onwards. Many schools start the GCSE curriculums in Y9, using modified past paper questions from the off. By Y10, teachers will be mentioning the phrase *in the exam* on a regular basis. By Y11, your child will probably hear these words in every lesson. Precise and published mark scheme requirements will mean that passing exams may feel to your child like a process of pleasing precise (and at times unfathomable) expectations.

Coupled with this, careers advice starts at KS3; by KS4, teenagers are encouraged to think about how they are preparing themselves for the world of work, logging their achievements on digital platforms via *skills trackers* and *achievement records,* or by signing up for work experience. Success also now seems to come with a price tag: are you paying out for tutors, revision guides, computers or school fees? If so, does this financial premium up the need for a return on the investment?

When I was at school, education was either free or much cheaper, exams were only a bit of what I did and I thought about job applications in my 20s when I was old enough to make them: exams were not the mantle for the whole school experience and I did not feel like my actions in Y8 had a noticed, logged and evaluated causal link to my future adult life. Your experience of school may or may not have been like mine, but the headline question is the same: if you were a child at school today, how different would your answers to the questions on p47 be?

> **Y11 Student:** *Learning the exam paper, finding a way to please the mark scheme – this feels about 50% of what we do. We talk about mark schemes and level ladders so often. Mark schemes are really inaccessible – there's so much jargon. So we spend a lot of time just trying to understand what the mark scheme is saying.*
>
> What's your immediate response to this? Does it seem similar or different to your memory of being at school?

Differences in perspective: Adults and teenagers

Even if schools hadn't changed at all, your perspective would still be different from your child's. You are an adult; they are a child. Your perspective is retrospective, shaped by a stable, processed memory of events that actually happened. Your child's experience is unfolding in real time, dominated by future-facing uncertainty full of *ifs* and *buts* about what might or might not happen in the exam.

Small children are so obviously different from adults that it's fairly straightforward to recognise that, for example, a long lunch is relaxing for adults but soul-crunchingly boring for a four-year-old. By the time a child is a teenager, however, the external differences reduce: maybe your child is now the same height as you, eats the same type of food, watches some of the same things on TV. As the overlap in shared experience increases, it can become harder to imagine how different these experiences might still feel to a child.

There will still be differences, however, even for shared experiences because of the three factors outlined below.

Factor #1: Experience of time

Think about how long a year feels to you as an adult; now think about how long it felt when you were 12 or 16. Exams are in view for much longer for children now than was the case 20 years ago. As parents, we need to keep thinking about how this extended run-up feels to a child, living through that period of time at their pace, not ours.

In addition, as parents our retrospective view of the exam experience accelerates our sense of the timeline. For a parent, the pathway from GCSE to A level to university may seem really quick and it may feel – retrospectively – like it went by in a flash: *before you know it you'll be sitting those exams!* This feels true enough to many parents; it rarely feels true to the child.

> **Student:** *I'd hear my parents say things like, 'You're lazy, you're not trying hard enough, if you fail these you won't get into uni.' It wasn't just about GCSEs to get into sixth form – the consequences were big – they stretched years ahead.*
>
> What is the impact of connecting something today with something else which is far away in the future? Does it make the consequences feel more or less manageable?

Factor #2: Experience of emotions

When was the last time you had a really surprising emotion? I don't mean when was the last time you were surprised *by* an emotion – we all know that emotions can arrive within us in a way that feels unexpected. I mean, when was the last time you felt something that you had never felt before and did not understand? In the intense developmental changes that adolescence brings, teenagers experience new emotions on a regular basis. They have feelings that arrive unexpectedly *and* which they don't recognise. This creates an additional complexity to how they feel about that emotion and how easily they can understand or explain that feeling, either to others or even to themselves.

Factor #3: Experience of self

As we grow up, eventually our identity settles down. It's not necessarily easier to find self-worth as an adult than as a teenager, but it's certainly easier to have self-knowledge. This has a bearing on our relationship with external judgement: if I go bowling with my kids, I'm no longer surprised if ball after ball ends up in the gutters. I can't throw straight: I might not like this fact, but I'm not surprised by it.

For teenagers, however, their sense of self is still in a state of flux: in particular, they don't know where they'll sit in the competitive hierarchy of exam grades, CV points, job applications. This means that the experience of being graded so definitively via test scores and exam results comes at a time where that definition is likely to cut deeply into their sense of self.

> **Y9 Student:** *My sense is that everyone in my year has at least a little bit of anxiety but those who identify as the cool kids try to suppress it a bit more – at least publicly. If they admit that they are nervous about exams then it's like a sign of weakness – they don't want to admit that there is something they can't do. Then there's the people at the top end – they're often very nervous because there's a lot more at stake.*
>
> How do grades shape identity and status at your child's school?

Differences in perspectives: Values

Some of the most painful areas of difference between a teenager's perspective and their parents' viewpoint often centre around values. If a parent doesn't understand why something matters to their child, it can leave their child feeling lonely, misunderstood and angry.

In the aftermath of Covid, I remember running a project for Y11 students at my school. As a senior leadership team, we were conscious of the way that remote school had left some students feeling invisible. Teaching had become more one-way: we were pushing resources and tasks at the students, but there were far fewer opportunities for the students to be seen or heard.

The project aimed to create a way to counteract this. It was based around a large display space in the middle of the school: I asked the year group to suggest images for us to put there. The only parameter was that the images should be something that was likely to be meaningful for others in their year group, too. Once the images had been chosen, I then asked the students to give their reactions to them. Comments were submitted anonymously and I printed out extracts to go up in the display space next to the images. The idea was that we'd create a space for the school community to see and hear what the students thought and felt about things which mattered to them.

As any teacher will tell you, if you create enough space for students to speak honestly, you'll realise that there are aspects to their life you'd never have understood without pausing to listen first. I'm no great lover of tech, and I'm usually the first to speak up about the need for boundaries around the online world, but I remember the jolt of reading one Y11's comment in relation to an image of a video game: *I wish my parents understood what gaming means to me.* I remember this comment now because it highlighted an area where I'd forgotten to think about different perspectives: I was so clear in my own mind about my own values that I hadn't paused to imagine why teenagers might feel very differently.

Daniel Siegel is the director of the Mindsight Institute and a leading writer on adolescent development. His book *Brainstorm: The Power and Purpose of the Teenage Brain* explores how adolescence and early adulthood is the phase in development where we experiment with and work out what is authentically meaningful to us. This can mean that a teenager feels surprised by what they suddenly care about or do not care about; their sense of their own priorities is unlikely to be neatly catalogued and, unlike their parents, their value system is unlikely to be settled and stable.

This means that a parent's sense of what a child *should* do and a child's feelings about what they *need* to do can be several steps away from each other. For the child, their values may be in a state of flux: it can be difficult for a child to navigate the differences between what they genuinely care about and what their parents tell them they *should* care about. As parents, sometimes we need to take a really searching look at how different our children might be from us and the different values they may have at any one point in time. If the differences feel painful to us, we need to remember that they are probably more painful and feel more isolating to our children.

> **Student:** *My mum is from a working-class background – both my mum and my dad believe that education is everything – I'm the first person in my family to go to uni. There's always this pressure to make the whole family proud and make their funding worth it.*
>
> How much is your child influenced by what you care about?
> Is this an easy question to answer?

In Parts 2 and 3 of this book, I'll be foregrounding the importance of supportive dialogue as a way to help your child through exams. It's worth noticing, though, what you're hoping to achieve as the end result of this dialogue: are you hoping that it'll help your child to come round to your point of view? Don't be surprised if your answer is *yes*. I'm fully committed to the principle that ultimately, my children need to live their own lives, but I'd be lying if I didn't say that it's a lot easier as a parent when my children agree with me.

Those are the easy conversations, though; much harder are the conversations where you're not on the same page. The real aim, therefore, of supportive dialogue is to create the space for differences to be recognised and understood. This will make it more straightforward to understand which expectations your child feels they should be meeting (see further, Chapter 1) and work out a way to help your child settle on a set of expectations or aspirations that are motivating, manageable, realistic and constructive.

☆ Questions to help you think about values

The questions below will help you think through your own values and start to explore where your child might be different. Often, where differences in values emerge between parents and children, it's comparatively temporary, but taking the time to be interested in these differences will make it easier for both of you to stay connected to each other even in the moments where you disagree about something. This will make it easier to find a game plan for the approach to exams that you both can agree to.

1. On a scale of 1–10, how important is formal education to you and why?
2. On a scale of 1–10, how important is formal education to your child and why? Is this a question you've already asked them, or do you need to guess what their answer would be?
3. Think about what you value in your child. Which of these aspects get as clearly and as regularly defined and labelled as their academic progress? If you asked your child what they think you value most in them, would their answer match the answer you've just given?
4. What does your child value or believe is most important in their life? Has that changed over time? How sure are you of your answer to this question?

I'm encouraging you to be alert at this stage to the potential differences in values because these can end up closing down conversations about how hard to work or what aspirations are suitable. This can make it harder for your child to find a balance in their priorities that feels right and sustainable. As I'll be discussing in later chapters, effective study habits are all about finding a realistic and appropriate balance in how your child spends their time.

It's also worth saying that there's no one-size-fits-all measure for how much it's appropriate for a parent to care about school grades: as the quotes below exemplify, teenagers can end up feeling out of kilter or unsupported if their parents either care a lot less or care a lot more about exam results than they do.

> **Y12 Student:** *My mum kept telling me my results wouldn't really matter that much but I think that in the past people didn't have to do as well – now grades are far more important. You have to do much better.*
>
> Do you think your child cares too much about their grades?
> How might it feel to your child if they think you don't understand why they care in this way?

> **Student:** *My parents really valued education. There was a focus on education as the only thing you're doing – for example, when I was doing my GCSEs my mum didn't want me to play hockey. If education is so important – if it's the only thing that seems to matter – then if you're feeling bad about school, you're feeling bad about your whole self.*
>
> Do you think your child doesn't care enough about school?
> Does that make it easier or harder for them to talk in detail about the parts of school that they find difficult or demotivating?

In this chapter, I've focused on the ways in which there may be differences in perspective between you and your child. Being alert to these differences will help you make the imaginative leap needed to understand your child's perspective better; this will make it easier for you to understand how to support them.

It's time now to start closing the gap between what you might expect your child's experiences to be like and the reality of what they actually are. Let's move on to Chapter 3: what are secondary schools really like today?

KEY IDEAS

- If your child feels that you do not understand their perspective, they are less likely to accept your help or advice.
- People typically use their own experience as a filter for understanding what someone else is talking about; this means that they can misunderstand how something feels to someone else.
- Schools have changed a lot in the last 20 years; your memories about taking exams may relate to an experience that was very different from your child's.
- Your perspective may also be different from your child's because, as an adult, you are likely to experience things in different ways. These differences relate to how adults experience time, how adults experience emotions and how familiar and settled an adult's sense of self is.
- Your child may have values that are different from your own: differences in values can be isolating and painful, especially for the child.
- Being alert to potential differences in perspective will help you have better conversations with your child; this will enable you to support them more effectively.

CHAPTER 3

Understanding what school is like today

Assistant Head, Teaching & Learning: *The stakes feel so high for the students – the difficulty is that the stakes are so high for schools as well. If we don't meet our progress markers, that's difficult for us, too – there's Ofsted, exam data for parents to access online – we're in a competitive market now.*

What is school actually like? Who knows the answer to a general question like this? Maybe no one; after all, each school is different. I think I'd argue the toss on this one, though: secondary schools look very different on the surface – different buildings, uniform, extracurricular provision, traditions, governance, budgets and so on – but all mainstream secondary schools centre their provision around the same basic experience of preparing students for external exams with very fixed and specific requirements. Each school has to push its pupils through the public exam pipeline and this means there are shared ingredients right at the heart of the school ecosystem.

As a parent, you need to know something about what's coming at your child 5 days a week, 35+ weeks a year. This chapter sets out the core ingredients that shape the secondary school experience today. I can't guarantee they'll apply to every child's experience to the same degree, but I'd be highly surprised if they weren't part of the mix for your child in some shape or form. I'm spending a whole chapter on this because if you don't understand what school is like for your child, it'll be very hard to know how to give them the practical and emotional support that they need.

Inspections and accountability

My own, subjective opinion is that – whatever the pros and cons of the current examination system – schools are much, much better than they used to be. I think they are kinder, more imaginative places, run with a clearer sense of purpose and a greater self-scrutiny than was the case when I first started teaching in the early 2000s. This is partly because the national agenda for schools has shifted: caring for a child – not just teaching them – is now core business. Schools have legal obligations to fulfil safeguarding responsibilities and PSHE programmes which address aspects of personal growth and development are compulsory.

The other reason for the improvements, however, is a more robust system of regular inspections by an external body – whether Ofsted in the maintained sector or ISI for the independent sector – and the fact that parents have access to exam results data and inspection reports.

This means that schools are much more accountable than they used to be. As a general principle, accountability improves standards. This principle is generally true, but this doesn't mean that accountability yields improvements in all areas, always. Sammy Wright's heartfelt and energetic book *Exam Nation* offers an excellent analysis of the cost of the accountability structures that schools operate within. Central within this is the idea of the marketisation of schools, creating winners and losers: parents can use inspection reports and exam results as a metric for choosing schools. This means that good schools attract the most invested families; this makes it easier for the good schools to thrive. Schools that are found to be failing attract fewer pupils; when pupil numbers go down, funding reduces. This makes it harder for these schools to improve.

The consequence of the marketisation of schools is that schools now face an existential need to be 'good'. *Nothing wrong with that*, you might say. But the devil is always in the detail and, for secondary school performance data, 'good' is measured predominantly by exam grades. Your child's grades matter to your child, but they also matter to the school.

All this is relevant to your child's potential exam stress because anxiety about outcomes is calibrated to how important those outcomes feel to the child. As Chapter 1 discussed, your child's beliefs about how much exams matter will depend, in part, on the values of the environment they find themselves in. Schools typically really do care about helping their students get the best grades they can: they want their students to access all the benefits of good grades for their own sake, but there's no getting away from the fact that these grades are also necessary for the school's success. It's a good thing when schools are committed to achieving the best results possible, but – as a parent – it's worth being aware of how this impacts the emotional temperature of the whole school experience.

The pressure on schools to get good results doesn't just affect how everyone feels about getting those grades. It also affects the decisions that schools make about how to teach and structure the curriculum and this, in turn, impacts what school will be like for your child. The next section will look at this now in more detail.

> **Science Teacher:** *In our context there's a bit of 'Our school is rubbish, everyone does rubbish, so what's the point?' We've had the Ofsted ranking to contend with – we're in special measures.*
>
> What sort of context is your child in? Is the basic assumption that the grades will be good or not?

The strategies used to raise grades

Schools work really hard to drive grades up. *Great,* you might say again, *that's what we want; we want to find the school that will be most effective at getting good grades.* Again, broadly speaking, I'd agree and professionally, I've given my all when I've been part of the process of raising outcomes. But we have to keep our eyes on the experience for the students; it's worth stepping back and clocking the side effects that the improvement regimen often brings with it.

I'm going to outline the techniques many schools use to get good results and then explain how this impacts the students. If you're keen to understand more about how teaching works, I hope this section will be interesting; if you want to get straight to the impact on the students, you'll find this on p61.

The recipe for raising standards often looks like this:

- **Syllabus content:** it takes several goes for material to enter the long-term memory; this means that many schools have adopted a loop-learning approach where, after content has been taught, students return to it several times before the exam.
- **Engagement:** engagement is the holy grail of effective teaching. If students concentrate in lessons and then do their classwork and homework with careful focus, they'll progress well. The best way to raise engagement is to notice and care when someone isn't engaged: this means embedding systems that follow up on missed homework and adopting classroom techniques designed to keep everyone listening, thinking and answering as much as possible. Many schools use teaching techniques such as *cold-calling* (where a teacher calls on a child for an answer rather than picking someone with their hand up) or *census checks* (where mini-whiteboards are used by everyone in the class to hold up an answer at the same time) or a fast series of short, timed tasks so that there's less opportunity to drift off in a daydream. All of these techniques are there to keep students

on their toes, to make sure they are involved regularly during the lesson and make it feel like they might be asked to respond at any moment.
- **Exam technique:** public exams like GCSEs and A levels are marked to very clear criteria. Mark schemes are published by the exam boards and these help teachers understand exactly how students can score marks. It also means that exam technique has become a central part of preparation: students need to learn *how* to answer questions in the way examiners are expecting.
- **Starting courses earlier:** during 2017–2020, the GCSE grading system changed from letters to numbers; at the same time, many GCSE syllabuses got bigger and contained more demanding content. The changes were designed to reduce grade inflation by making it harder to get higher grades, but it also meant that many schools decided to give their students a better chance at those grades by starting GCSE content earlier.
- **Senior management checks:** to raise standards, senior management teams need to do regular data checks, reviewing outcomes for students across different classes, checking that the results are as expected and intervening if something looks problematic. This only works, however, if parallel classes sit the same internal assessments at the same time, and this is one of the reasons why many schools now run several waves of whole-year-group assessments within the same academic year. This means that, in order to raise exam results, children often end up sitting formal exams on a very regular basis.

The ingredients mentioned above generate better results: this is a good thing. But they also shift the experience for the student. Let's look at this now.

The impact on the students #1: Repetition
Education has become more repetitive: I now teach the same content several times to the same students. This means they know it better, but it also makes it more boring. This reaches a peak in the GCSE years,

which – developmentally – is the time when many adolescents are hungry for new experiences. It creates an awkward conflict between what their instinctive development is craving and what they are told they need to take seriously and care about.

> **Y12 Student:** *The main feeling during GCSEs? Bored – just the same thing every day.*
>
> - Does your child seem bored by school? How does this affect their attitude to work?
> - When does your child seem most energetic? What does this show you about what interests and motivates them?

The impact on the students #2: Energy

Strategies to increase engagement create better outcomes, but they also increase how much is asked of students during each day. If the school is doing its job well, your child will be concentrating in every lesson. I'm 100% an advocate of maximising engagement in the classroom – your child should be working hard when they are at school – but it may impact how ready they are to be focused, engaged and responsive to adults when they are at home. As later chapters will explore, this is something which is worth being imaginative about when working out what type of support to offer them during the exam years.

If your child's school runs multiple waves of school exams each year, this will also impact your child's energy. Assessment weeks are really tiring, and especially so if they impact how much time your child has to rest and recharge at the weekend or during school holidays.

> **Y10 Student:** *Sometimes when you get home from school you just want to get back to a place where nothing is demanded of you.*
>
> - What does your child need most when they get home?

The impact on students #3: Complexity and rigidity

Public exams are marked to a set of very specific criteria. This means they can be marked fairly and consistently, but it also means that students now have to learn content *and* the expectations of the exam. When I turned up to my History GCSE in the 1990s, I knew some facts and figures. Today, I would need to remember facts, figures *and* a whole set of instructions about exactly how to answer different types of questions. This means that preparing for exams has become much more complicated.

Specific mark scheme criteria also mean that preparing to pass an exam has become a very rigid process. In order to be clear and consistent, exam mark schemes need to be precise and prescriptive. What this means for the student is that their answer needs to be *exactly* one type of thing. This creates a rigidity and difficulty that has nothing to do with how easy or difficult the subject content is. The margin of tolerance for what 'right' looks like now is very small indeed and – as later chapters will discuss in more detail – this is highly relevant to how stressed your child will feel about their chances of landing the marks.

This consequence is compounded by starting syllabuses earlier. Including exam practice right from the start means that students have time to become familiar with exam expectations, but it also means they spend a long time feeling like getting it 'right' looks like only one sort of thing. This is why I'll be talking so much in Part 2 and Part 3 about the need for parents to provide a counterbalance to help their children remember that *doing OK* in general isn't as fixed and rigid as *doing OK* in an exam.

> **Y13 Student:** *GCSE was quite formulaic – especially sciences – you didn't have to understand, you just had to memorise answers. For A level, you still need to understand what the examiner wants – learning the content isn't enough. Hitting the criteria is about 70% of what I think about.*
>
> Have you heard your child talk about exam technique? How old were they when they first mentioned this? What impact does it have on the way they learn and how they think?

The impact on students #4: Stretching out the timeline

Starting things earlier is great if, for example, you are training for a marathon. But for children, starting things earlier means starting things younger and stretching out the timeline during which exams are clearly in view. The run-up to public exams lasts for multiple years: two years for sixth form courses but for GCSEs it's probably a three-year pathway starting in Y9. When your child finally sits GCSEs aged 16, they'll have been thinking about them for nearly a fifth of their life – maybe longer. Viewed as a proportion of their existence, the exam-marathon is enormous.

Stretching the timeline means that teenagers hear about exams a lot. This can have several consequences: for some students, it makes exams feel disproportionately important; for other students, hearing about exams again and again increases the exam fatigue, adding to the risk that students disengage and switch off.

> **English Teacher:** *I've been teaching for 35 years. The KS3 curriculum used to be all about breadth and trying things out. Now it's much more a matter of preparing them for next steps. Lots of schools are starting GCSE courses in Y9. Increasingly they are no longer exploring and creating and dabbling at KS3; it's much more about getting ready for KS4.*
>
> - Do you think deadlines, targets and assessments become more or less stressful if they've been talked about for years?

> **Y11 Student:** *After Christmas in Y11 we had lots of assemblies about GCSEs – maybe every other week – they focused on revision. There was a feeling of we've heard all this before.*
>
> - Repetition makes a message familiar, but it also impacts the way someone feels about the message. How do your children respond when they hear the same thing again and again?

In Part 2 and Part 3 I'll be giving guidance about how you can help your child thrive in the context of school as it is today. This guidance will help your child get the benefit of all the strategies schools use to raise results while avoiding the potentially negative consequences outlined above.

Before we move on, however, there is one final piece of groundwork to do. Healthy and effective levels of motivation, engagement and flexibility will be central throughout the advice in Part 2 and Part 3, but they all depend on your child having enough time and energy. So our last piece of groundwork is this: what sort of pressures are there on your child's time?

Time pressure: Is your child too busy?

I'd also say schools today are much busier now than they used to be. They're certainly busier places for teachers, but I'm pretty sure they're busier for the students as well. Raising engagement in classrooms means that students are busier, doing more during lessons. Learning mark-scheme expectations *and* content means that preparation is busier, with more things to think about. Running more waves of assessment means that there are more moments in the year when it's time to start revising *again*, creating a busier feel to the rhythm of the year.

☆ **Working out if your child is too busy**
How busy is your child? Is this question easy to answer? You could have a go at doing some sums via the questions below and then use the same questions to think back to your own childhood: how busy were you and how did this feel? If your child is more or less busy than you were, is this likely to feel more or less OK than your level of adolescent busyness felt to you?

1. How many hours a week does your child spend at school?
2. How many hours a week does your child spend travelling to and from school?
3. How many hours a week does your child spend on homework?

4. How many hours a week does your child spend on extracurricular activities?
5. How many hours a week does your child spend on helping out around the house?
6. How many hours a week does your child spend on socialising?
7. How many hours a week does your child spend in a way that is unstructured and free?

These sums might throw up some thought-provoking truths. I'm not alone in the teaching community in thinking that a very large number of children are far too busy, especially in the evenings, with a pile of extracurricular commitments that put an unhealthy toll on their available time and energy.

> **Academic Lead for Y11:** *We encourage extracurricular because we want the students to have a good work-life balance, but we do try and get them to think about how busy they are. Sometimes they can find it hard to give something up. This might be because of a perceived feeling of disappointing someone – maybe their teacher or their parents perhaps.*
>
> Does your child find it straightforward to give something up? If they don't, why do you think this is?

☆ Is there enough time?

If we're going to assess whether or not children are too busy, we need to be clear about what they need time for. If your child doesn't have a reasonable amount of time ring-fenced for their homework then that's a straightforwardly clear metric. Homework matters and if they need more time for it, then something else probably needs to go (see further, Chapter 5.)

Homework is an easy metric because it's so obviously relevant to progress, but what about the metrics that are less clearly defined? What about your child's need to decompress, to have space just to process the maelstrom of the day? As discussed above, at school, children should be working hard. This is good, but its counterbalance is they probably need more time to switch off after school than you might think.

> **Y12 Student:** *Exhaustion is a big thing – at the very beginning I felt so much stress, but then as it went on I was really burnt out, I ended up stopping caring. I put a lot less effort into it.*
>
> When your child gets too tired, how does their behaviour change?

There's a caveat to the questions I set out on p65: they suggest that there are separate categories for how your child spends their time. This used to be true, but social media means that the goalposts have shifted. When my generation went home from school, socialising stopped unless someone phoned or knocked on the door. There were clear boundaries. For today's teenagers, their social life runs pretty much 24-7. Notifications are pinging at all hours of the day and the night.

This also means that the answer to how much time is spent freely is much more complex than it seems at first sight. If your teenager is sitting on the sofa not doing much, it looks like they're free. But if their phone is in their hand, they're probably not: their attention is probably being diverted hither and thither by the attention-grabbing mechanisms of the various algorithms that are designed to keep pulling them in. This means that their brain is not roaming freely, it isn't processing and moving through the things that it needs to; instead it's being distracted by stuff which is designed to be diverting, at a pace that is calibrated to allow no pause for the brain to resume its own agenda.

> **Student:** *You want to seem like you're available to your friends so that people don't think you're a horrible person. Most people don't manage to set boundaries. In Y13 I had a friend who had really serious screen time apps to put boundaries in. I respected her but it was also really hard because her WhatsApp limit would kick in and she'd disappear from the conversation. I'd feel that I wanted to talk to her but then she wasn't there.*
>
> Does your child find it straightforward to set boundaries around how they use social media?

Anyone who has ever done any serious fitness work will know that strength development depends upon rest periods. So here's a serious question: when does your child really, truly get to rest? When can they switch off from everything that's going on at school? When is their phone out of sight and out of mind? When are they free from someone else's *do this, do that* set of instructions? And – most importantly of all – are you certain there's enough space left to make sure they do not feel overwhelmed by everything they're supposed to be thinking about?

> **11–18 SENDCO:** *Sometimes you only get to see the outside: the child is sitting in a lesson, nodding along, the teacher thinks they're OK. But the child is maybe thinking about all their homework, the different lessons that day, the test coming up, what their friends said on WhatsApp. They're functionally frozen. They look like they're engaged in the lesson but actually they're not processing it at all – they are overwhelmed by so much going on in their heads. They're overwhelmed by all the competing pressures of everything that's happening that day.*
>
> What are the competing pressures for your child? How many different things do they feel they need to be good at?

If you asked your child to write a list and tell you which pressures felt the heaviest, what do you think they would say? How sure are you that your child's answers would match your predictions?

KEY IDEAS

- Schools are under pressure to drive results up: this means that students often learn the same syllabus content several times over and practise exam questions repeatedly, often sitting multiple sets of formal assessments each year.
- Exams are marked to very precise criteria; this means that students need to learn exam technique as well as subject content.
- Preparing for exams now lasts longer than it used to. In addition, exam preparation has become more repetitive and more complex.
- Social media means that socialising has become less boundaried and more time-consuming.
- Many teenagers find it harder to do well because they are too busy and too tired.

PART

How to help your child: Key techniques

> The techniques in Part 2 focus on how you can reduce the risks that your child becomes problematically affected by exam stress. These techniques are relevant at any stage in the journey through secondary school. They also provide the foundation for the age-specific guidance that I'll be giving in Part 3.

> If your child is already affected by exam stress, they may need help with the consequences of this, such as raised heart rate, tension and nausea. If you need further guidance on relaxation techniques, deep-breathing exercises, or other ways to help your child with the physical and psychological consequences of stress, there is **advice available on the NHS website**. If you have concerns about your child's well-being, it is best to reach out for professional advice at an early stage (see further, p182).

CHAPTER 4

Creating constructive conversations about school

Student: *I think one of the barriers to speaking to my parents about my relationship with schoolwork was that I didn't really understand it myself.*

Why are teenagers often so reluctant to talk about school? Is it just because they've *become really grumpy* or *have lost the ability to answer in anything other than grunts*? Or are the reasons more complex? As parents, sometimes we forget how difficult it can be for a teenager to explain what's really going on: it can be hard for a teenager to find the words to describe new and potentially painful experiences. Often, feelings of shame or embarrassment make it hard for a teenager to talk openly to their parents.

In this chapter, I'll be focusing on creating constructive conversations about school. These conversations will help you – and your child – to understand what's going on and work out what to do next when problems arise. I'll be explaining why conversations about school can get derailed, disintegrating into a series of angry shouts, slammed doors and *I told you I don't want to talk about it*. I'll be setting out two key strategies for you to use to create better conversations, highlighting the importance of listening for long enough and outlining the principles that will help you respond effectively.

> **Y10 Student:** *Every student has different levels of stress and they are aiming for different grades, so what they need to do to deal with their stress levels will be different for everyone.*
>
> Many teenagers talk more to their friends than their parents, missing out on the support that their parents could provide. What support can you offer that a friend can't?

Why conversations about homework, tests or exams can be difficult

Your child's experience of school will be a mixture of concrete facts that are easy to understand – such as *I had Maths today* – and very amorphous feelings that aren't easy to understand at all, such as *my stomach feels tense and I've got a headache and I feel like I need to shout at someone but I don't know why*. When your child is thinking about exams, there may be a double dose of complexity: they may find the exam requirements challenging and they'll need to process whatever feelings the prospect of exams is producing. Constructive conversations are an essential ingredient in helping your child manage this complexity, but they are not always easy to achieve. Let's think now about why this is.

Difficulty #1: Conversations often get tense

Tests and exams are a moment where, suddenly, lots of people care about how a child does: the teacher will set expectations about what answers should look like, you may have expectations about what grade you'd like your child to get, your child will have their own expectations about how the exam will – or should – go, and there'll probably be plenty of chat between classmates about who's going to get what. Your child will be in the middle of this and unless, by some miracle, all these expectations magically align, it'll be like a system of pulleys, all pulling in slightly different directions. It's not surprising that it gets fraught.

This means that conversations about schoolwork that get anywhere close to the powder keg of *are the marks high enough, has the homework been done well enough, are you working hard enough* can get very tense, very quickly. *They never tell me anything about school*: I hear this at parents' evenings all the time. There's a high risk that conversations about schoolwork feel abrasive for the teenager: it's often easier for them to pull away and close the conversations down. *It's fine, stop hassling me, I told you – it's fine.*

The powder keg doesn't just belong to the child; conversations about schoolwork can be painful, frustrating or infuriating for the parent too. *Are the marks OK?* Behind this concern is usually the wish to help and support. If a teenager doesn't seem to want their parent's attention or advice, this can feel like rejection or a lack of respect; the temptation can be to weigh in more strongly, asserting parental authority more vigorously, saying things like *Don't walk away from me while I'm talking to you! This matters and you need to take it seriously!*

If conversations start to get brittle, anger starts to get inked into the layers of memory. The pattern embeds and the steps become too familiar: muscle memory means that reactions get ingrained, everyone flies off the handle and it can start to feel impossible to talk about schoolwork at all. Many parents have described to me how adrift they feel when this happens. Often the parent feels left on the sidelines, watching while disappointing marks roll in or problematic behaviours continue, but feeling like there's not much they can do to shift things.

> **Assistant Head, Teaching & Learning:** *The parents will say that the kids say, 'You don't know this, you can't help me with this.' This raises the stress levels massively – the parents are worried but they don't feel like they can help.*
>
> - Does your child listen to your advice about school? If not, how do you respond when they don't?

Difficulty #2: Creating space for emotions

If conversations about school become high-octane emotionally, this brings an additional difficulty. These emotions become part of the conversation and it becomes necessary to navigate them.

Unfortunately – from a parent's perspective – the child's feelings can seem inappropriate. Many conversation patterns end up pushing these feelings to one side. If your child gets angry, it's easy to criticise them for this: *You need to stop shouting! Can't we just have a sensible conversation about school?* If a child gets very upset, adults often try to reassure by suggesting that the feeling is disproportionate: *Don't cry – you're overreacting – you don't need to get this upset.* A similar thing often happens when a child is worried: *Don't worry – it'll be fine!*

These responses are well-meaning, but they implicitly invalidate the emotional response; this closes down the opportunity for your child to tell you more about why they are feeling this way. The problem with this is that emotions land uninvited and they are often confusing and difficult, especially for a teenager. Removing the chance for a child to talk about – and think about – what they are feeling makes it harder for the child to process and move through their emotions. In the long run, this makes it harder for the child to understand and be calm about the natural emotional responses that school often produces.

> **Counselling and Mental Health Leader:** *I do a lot of training with teachers at my school in active listening: whatever the young person says, the first thing to do is to validate the feeling. For example, say something like 'I can see that you are really anxious or I can hear that you are really worried right now'. It's important to acknowledge what the child has said – not to push it away too fast.*
>
> How do you respond when your child has an emotion which doesn't seem valid to you?

Difficulty #3: Finding words for emotions

Even for adults, thinking and talking about emotions can be tricky. Words cut things into neat shapes, distinguishing x from y via a distinct label: *table, chair, day, night*. Feelings aren't neat at all: *joy, delight, satisfaction, contentment, happiness, cheerfulness* – the dividing lines between these aren't crisp. It's even harder in the context of painful emotions: the natural instinct is to flinch away rather than focus forensically on what it is that's so upsetting. Think about a basic feeling of anger and the range of hard-to-see ingredients that can be swilling around within it, such as *disappointment, shame, envy, embarrassment, guilt, rejection, surprise* or *betrayal*.

The difficulty in thinking or talking about feelings is compounded by the physical structures in the brain. Emotions arise from the limbic regions in the middle of the brain; language is the preserve of the cortical areas that form the outermost layers of the brain. Putting feelings into words requires using two different areas of the brain and it's not always straightforward for both regions to be active at once.

The brain develops from the central brain stem outwards and – in line with the order of development – there's a hierarchy between brain regions. If strong emotions surge, it can be difficult for the rational, verbal cortical areas to stay engaged: this is why it is genuinely difficult – sometimes impossible – to think rationally about anything if feelings are running high.

For teenagers in particular, it's harder still. For a start, many of their feelings are new, tied up with experiences they haven't had before and impulses which are connected to adolescent development: this means they have to learn the labels to describe them. Then there's the fact that the rational area of the brain, the prefrontal cortex, undergoes major redevelopment during adolescence. This redevelopment facilitates, in the long term, better connections within the brain and the ability to integrate one brain function with another more efficiently. This enables the types of thinking that are a sign of maturity, but – in the short term – the restructuring in the prefrontal cortex means that it's sometimes much harder to bring its capacities into the mix and especially so when emotions are high. Sometimes when a teenager says they don't want to talk about something, it's because – in the moment when their emotions are surging – they really can't manage to feel and think at the same time. This is why teenagers often need time, space and empathy so that their feelings can settle *before* the talking begins. If you'd like to read more about the changes in a teenager's brain, *Blame my Brain* by Nicola Morgan offers a very clear summary.

Difficulty #4: Listening for long enough

My parents wouldn't understand. Whenever a teenager has told me about something difficult in their lives, I always ask them if they've told their parents. If they haven't, I ask them why: *they wouldn't understand* is the reason I hear more than any other. It's not always true – often the parent wants nothing more than to understand – but it's usually based on the belief that their parent won't listen patiently and for long enough for the child to feel they've had a chance to explain things properly.

As a parent, listening can be surprisingly difficult. Our habits as parents tend to be shaped very early on and they are often driven by the instinct to respond as quickly as possible. When a baby cries, the impulse is to act immediately, to try to do something to make it better. The toddler years can cement this: after all, toddlers don't exactly choose their moment carefully for a meltdown and there isn't always the time to stop, listen, think and pause before responding if your three-year-old is screaming on the floor in the supermarket.

During the teenage years it can also be difficult to listen properly before responding. Families are busy: extracurricular commitments, work emails, checking in about homework, getting on with cooking or tidying or laundry and the seemingly endless admin of family life – all of this can end up running concurrently in the evenings. Everyone's tired and – as you'll know – you can't exactly diarise an important conversation with your children. Teenagers tell you things on their schedule, not yours. Many parents find that some of the most important work of parenting is done at the most inconvenient times. The parental impulse is often focused on making things better and finding a solution as quickly as possible; this can make it tempting to hurry through the explanations in an attempt to find the answer sooner rather than later.

The challenge of really listening to children is made more complex because early interactions with our children are preverbal: very young children can't use words to tell us what they want. We have to interpret their behaviour and come to our own conclusions. There's a thin line between this and making assumptions. If the transition from nonverbal to verbal communication was a nice noticeable change at a clearly defined moment, maybe it would be easier to adjust our habits, but it's not.

Communication between parent and child evolves over time; a child gradually gets better at using words to express what has happened and how they feel about it, but it's a slow, hazy process and – pre-secondary school – parents still have to do a fair bit of reading between the lines to work out what's going on. Unless these habits are consciously readjusted, by the time a child is a teenager, the impulse to *assume* you know what your child means and jump right in with the advice is the result of a set of behavioural patterns that have been running for 10 years or more.

> **Assistant Head, Teaching & Learning:** *There's so much challenge that some of our kids face. I had one kid come to me before an exam – he hadn't slept because they had a bedbug infestation, but he still sat that exam. We very rarely stop to pause and think about the story within each person. They have a back story – we often don't have time for this back story – and the kids often learn to not express their back story.*
>
> It can be hard for teachers to know each child's back story, but it can be equally hard for parents to know what is going on in the background. Which parts of your child's back story are you least likely to know about?

Why problems make conversations harder

Teenagers often find it difficult to talk to their parents about their lives in general, but sometimes it becomes even harder for them if something's going wrong at school. I'd say there are three main reasons for this.

Reason #1: Teenagers often don't want to ask for help

Young children usually enjoy it when their parents help them; it's an affirming, reassuring indicator of availability and love. For a teenager, it's a different story: receiving help from their parents can feel embarrassing and a sign that the teenager isn't up to the task. This is especially true for schoolwork because every teenager knows they're supposed to get it right on their own. In addition, talking about something means facing it head-on; for many teenagers it's easier to look away, distracting themselves by thinking about something else rather than opening themselves up to admit – and really feel – the double-dimensioned pain of whatever it is that is troubling them and their discomfort at not being able to fix it on their own.

Reason #2: Advice gets heard as criticism

If schoolwork isn't going well, teenagers often feel at fault or inadequate. This is because they'll see other people in their class doing the same piece of work: if it's going badly, they'll be aware that other people are probably getting higher marks. If a student feels that it's possible to do better, they'll probably also feel that the limiting factor is that something is lacking in them. This is exacerbated by the fact that the usual response is to talk about what the student should be doing differently. Conversations about school do need to address what could – or should – be done differently, but it's important to remember that the feelings of shame or embarrassment that this creates are likely to make it more difficult for a teenager to be honest with their parents.

Advice can be surprisingly difficult for teenagers to receive, and especially from their parents. If the starting point for a conversation is that the child feels at fault, and the parent then weighs in right away with what they should do now, it's hard for a teenager not to hear this as *I'm helping you out here because you aren't able to sort this on your own*. No matter how unintended, parental advice gets served up with an implicit side salad of *here's another thing you might be about to get wrong if I don't intervene*. When advice gets filtered through teenage ears, it often gets heard as criticism.

Reason #3: The problem feels bigger

If something is going wrong and a teenager is unhappy, they need the situation to become more manageable, not more overwhelming and out of control. The way parents respond, however, can make a situation feel worse. Take friendship issues, for example: a child tells their parent that their friend has been mean to them. If the parent picks up the phone, talks to the other parent, contacts the school, asks for a meeting, the situation is suddenly *bigger* than it was before.

This is often why teenagers are reticent to talk to their parents: they fear doing something that might make a painful, unmanageable situation more visible, more complicated, more emotionally charged and somehow bigger than when no one else knew about it. *Don't make such a big thing of it. No, I don't want you to contact the school. I wish I hadn't said anything.*

> **Student:** *It felt hard to try and explain to someone else how bad things were without them worrying. It feels like if you tell your parents what's going on they will think and act differently around you, worry more – it's not what you need. I think I was very scared of my parents' reaction. I didn't think that they would be angry or shout. I thought they would be scared and not know what to do themselves. I think that when you're struggling, you think 'I can control this' – particularly when it's your parents, you worry that if you tell them then it'll be out of your control.*

> What might your child worry about when it comes to the way you'd react if there's a problem? Would they expect you to get angry? Or could there be something else that might hold them back?
>
> Would they feel anxious about upsetting, worrying or disappointing you?
>
> Would they worry that they'd end up locked into next steps that they didn't feel ready for?

All this means that if a teenager is going to find the courage to be honest about something difficult, they need to believe that their parent will listen calmly and patiently *before* launching into what to do next. This is why the first strategy below focuses on the techniques that will help you listen for long enough first so that your child will be able to tell you what's going on.

★ Key Strategy #1: Listening for longer

If your child is already some way into adolescence, you've probably experienced a moment where you feel that, as a parent, you *can't get anything right*. Teenagers are very sensitive to how their parents react, as we've discussed above; this means that – no matter how well-intentioned the response – conversations can derail very quickly.

The first key strategy, therefore, is to learn to listen for longer first and hold back on reacting, even if this feels different from the way you responded when your child was younger. When a small child falls off a swing and grazes their knee, we pick them up, clean the wound, put a plaster on and *make it better*. Small children come to us for quick solutions, but it's different for teenagers and especially so when it comes to exam stress. This is because:

- **Exams are inevitably stressful.** We can't just clean it up, put a plaster on, make it go away. Instead, our job as parents is to help

our children think about, understand and find a route through this stress.
- **As children get older, they need to become more independent.** If we jump in with solutions too quickly, we don't create enough space for children to become more confident that they can manage difficult situations for themselves.

Sometimes, what teenagers need most is the opportunity to talk, explain and make sense of what is happening. They need an adult to listen and be there as a sounding board, but they're not looking for that adult to jump in and tell them what to do straightaway. There's still a role for your advice and guidance, but the pacing is likely to be different from when your child was younger.

In practice, this means remembering the following techniques:

- **Pause before you respond** in case there's something else that your child is about to say.
- **Check that your child has finished:** *Is there anything else you'd like to tell me or are you ready for me to say something?*
- **Restate what you've heard and see if it's right:** *It sounds like you're worried that you'll get a worse grade than last time – or have I misunderstood what you said? If so, could you help me try to understand it better?*
- **Gently see if your child can explain things more deeply:** it's important not to push a conversation beyond what your child can manage, but – if your child seems willing to engage with this – asking a bit more will help you and your child understand the situation better. You might find exploratory questions useful, such as the following examples, but remember to ask just one question at a time and stop if your child has had enough. If your child feels bombarded, they're likely to pull away.
  - *Are you surprised by this or do your feelings make sense to you?*
  - *Have you felt this way before? What's similar or different between then and now?*

- *Do you think your teacher wants you to feel this way? What do you think their perspective on this would be?*
- *Do you think any of your friends are in a similar situation? In what ways is your situation similar or different to theirs?*
- *What do you think you need from me right now? Is there anything you're hoping that I won't do?*
- **Respect your child's need to pause:** conversations can be hard work for a teenager; if your child says that they've had enough, it's important to respect this. *OK, I see that you'd like to pause things here, so let's stop. But, if you feel ready to talk again later, I'd really appreciate the chance to understand things better and see how I can help and support you.*

Child and Adolescent Psychotherapist: *Listening without judgement: this is so important and it means don't offer a solution straightaway. That shuts down the conversation. Children need the space and time to talk things through.*

When your child tells you about something that has gone wrong, what's your first response? Do you pause to listen further or do you try to fix the problem straightaway?
What are the factors in your context that can make it difficult to listen for long enough?

Listening for longer will help you *and* your child understand the situation better, but it's got one more important benefit: it's much easier for a teenager to be open to advice if they've had enough time to do their own thinking and feel properly understood first. If you don't listen for long enough, your child is much more likely to reject your advice, either because they feel it isn't relevant, or because – in their efforts to try to be understood – they'll keep trying to reassert their viewpoint. If you feel that your child doesn't listen to you, it may be because they don't feel you've listened properly to them first.

> **Student:** *I think the dialogue at home makes a big difference. My brother and I were very different: my brother needed more of the pressure whereas I needed more calming down.*
>
> What's your usual approach to giving advice? Do you have general advice that you always fall back on? Or do you focus on understanding the specifics of a situation patiently first so that you can adjust your advice in a way that fits your child's needs?

★ Key Strategy #2: How to respond

Listening is the first step, but – after you've listened for long enough – you'll need to respond. How you do this will depend on the age of your child: as children get older, conversation patterns need to shift and develop. The older the child, the more a parent needs to step back and listen; the younger the child, the more likely it is that the child will still be looking for the parent to swoop in and help. The age-specific chapters in Part 3 offer advice that is calibrated to different school year groups, but the principles below will help you think about the structures and responses that create constructive conversations at any age.

- Does the response take an interest in your child's feeling, encouraging your child to describe it further, strengthening their ability to understand and process their emotions?
- Does the response acknowledge the reality of your child's emotion, helping them feel understood, or does it bat it away by suggesting that the feeling is somehow inappropriate?
- Does the response create the space and empathy needed for your child's feelings to surface and settle *before* talking and thinking about what to do next? If your child needs to cry – or be angry – is there space for them to do this *before* discussing why they were feeling like this or what they should do next?

- Does the response make the situation bigger and more problematic or does it make it more normal and more manageable?
- Does the response stay focused on your child's perspective and the aspects of the situation that they can do something about?
- Does the response enable your child to develop their own skills in working out what to do next, or does it jump straight to advice that implies your child was getting something wrong or wouldn't have known what to do?
- Does the response focus only on trying to make sure something goes well or does it help your child think about how they'd handle the situation even if something goes wrong?

Potentially counterproductive responses

Sometimes, as parents, we're so used to responding in a particular way that we don't pause to think about how that response might land. The examples and analysis below will help you think about the potentially negative impact of some types of response; this will help you decide whether you want to respond in that way or not. On p89, I'll be sharing ideas about ways to respond that may be more constructive.

All the example responses below come from the same starting point: the parent wants to help their child do well. They are all well-intentioned and come from a place of love and support but the messaging the child hears may be different from what the parent intended. As will be the case for all the conversation samples in this book, the analysis is designed to encourage reflection about how a child may hear their parents' words. The analysis is not a hard and fast rule book because different children respond in different ways. Some teenagers are much more sensitive to criticism than others; some need much longer to think about emotions while others will want to get into the specifics of what to do next much more quickly. As a parent, you'll know the specifics of your context and the degree to which the analysis is relevant to the dynamics of your own conversations. As explained at the start of this book, it's useful to maintain a degree of healthy scepticism so that you can separate the suggestions which resonate with your context from the suggestions which don't.

If you find yourself unsure about whether or not your child would hear you in the way I've outlined below, it'd be worth discussing the conversation sample with your child and seeing what they think. They may or may not agree with the analysis: either way, it'll be a useful thing to do because your understanding of how a conversation feels from your child's perspective will probably be clearer afterwards.

I'm worried about my Maths test tomorrow.

- *You don't need to worry – it'll be fine!* This is a standard, quick-fire response. The intention is to reassure, but the side-message is that the worry is inappropriate: if there's no need to worry then the child shouldn't be worrying. This can problematise the feeling, making it harder for the child to open up further.
- *How much revision have you done? What mark do you think you'll get?* This response goes straight to the detail, asking for a quantified, rational response. Getting into the detail is constructive, but your child may not be able to manage it straightaway. Their feelings may need to surface then settle before the thinking can begin. If your child is worried, they may need to tell you they're worried and then take some time to pause and breathe deeply so that they return to a place that's calm enough for them to start to discuss things in more detail.
- *I loved Maths at school – how about I help you with your revision?* This response offers support, but it overshadows it by foregrounding a potentially unhelpful comparison between child and parent, unintentionally suggesting that *this wasn't a problem for me! Look – you're not measuring up to how I was at school.*
- *I used to feel this way too! But it was never as bad as I thought it'd be.* This response opens with empathy, but it runs the risk of closing down the conversation because it moves too quickly to the idea of *it's going to be fine!* It doesn't leave the space to explore what happens if it isn't fine; this reduces the scope for the child to see how they could manage the situation even if the worst-case scenario lands.

Everyone's better at French than me.
- *This is the first I've heard of it! Why hasn't the school been in touch about this?* This response increases the problem, taking the initial situation and throwing in parental surprise and criticism of the school as well. The child may be left feeling that telling their parent has made things more complicated and more emotionally charged, rather than simpler and more manageable.
- *Why didn't you tell me sooner that you were struggling? If you let yourself get behind, it's harder to catch up.* This response escalates the problem by adding blame into the mix. The message to the child is that they are now at fault for three things, not one: doing badly at French, not telling their parent, and creating a situation that is going to be more difficult to resolve than it should be. The child is likely to feel worse, not better: this creates the risk they withdraw or get angry.
- *You're going to need to work harder to sort this out. I'm going to phone the school tomorrow to ask them for more work.* This response goes straight to problem-solving without any space for understanding the feelings or listening carefully first. It also implies that the child won't be able to come up with a solution; this removes the opportunity for the child to develop their own ideas about how to improve things.
- *Do you need a tutor? We can do this but it's expensive, so if we pay for tutoring, you'd better not waste it!* This response raises the ante: the child starts by feeling like they've failed and the solution puts the premium for success even higher. This increases the risk factor: if the child gets a tutor and *still* can't do French, they risk disappointing their parent or feeling guilty that they've wasted their parent's money. This may make it harder for the child to be honest in the future if they're *still* finding French difficult.

I failed my History assessment.
- *You're going to need to work harder for the next one! You're at secondary school now and you need to start taking work seriously.* This response opens with direct criticism, telling the child that there's fault in

their attitude as well as their grade. It gives a general instruction to do better but it doesn't help with the specifics of how to achieve this. Opening with criticism makes it more uncomfortable for the child to reflect on their attitude, meaning that it may be harder for them to work out how to study more effectively.

- *How badly? What did everyone else get?* This draws comparisons with others, shifting the focus away from the parts of the situation that are specific to the child. As Chapter 8 will discuss, teenagers constantly compare themselves to others, often in a raw and self-critical way; this can impact morale and their readiness to work harder. It doesn't encourage the child to focus on the bits of the situation that they can do something about; how others do is not something that your child has any control over.

- *I'm really disappointed to hear this. You told me at the weekend you'd revised. What happened?* This increases the problem by adding parental disappointment into the mix. It also implies that the parent thinks the child has been lying, making it harder for the child to feel that their words will be believed in this conversation.

I can't go to bed because I haven't finished my English homework and my teacher says that if I don't finish it I'll be in detention but I can't do it and it's a stupid homework anyway and I hate school.

- *Don't you realise it's already 9pm on a Sunday – we don't have time for this now! Why did you leave it so late? I told you to get your homework done this morning!* This response piles on the criticism, taking the child's worry about detention and increasing it with criticism about choices which now can't be undone. It doesn't help the child work out what to do next in order to find a route through this situation.

- *Don't you know that detentions go on your record? Do you have any idea how embarrassing it is for me when the school phones me up to tell me you're not working properly?* This response takes the child's fear of detention and compounds it, embedding the idea that, yes, this problem is a big one. It doesn't leave any space for helping the child work out how to find a constructive route from detention to something better in the future.

- *Your teacher shouldn't be making you feel this way – it's far too much pressure. I'm going to email her right away and tell her we need a meeting about this. She's obviously setting the wrong type of work.* This response goes to the other extreme; it implies that the situation shouldn't have occurred in the first place. It suggests that it's inappropriate to be in a position of finding something difficult; it does nothing to help the child accept that difficulty is natural at times and part of growing up is to learn how to navigate this.

★ A constructive approach to conversations

Constructive responses are likely to contain some of the following ingredients. They are relevant to any of the situations outlined above, but it's best to think of this list as a selection box. The suggestions are unlikely all to be needed at once, but they are there to offer a range of ideas for how to respond. You'll see that I've included reminders to hold back and listen for long enough first since – as discussed on p81 – this is a central part of the process.

As with the examples above, it's probably a good idea to discuss these with your child: what's their view on whether they'd find these approaches constructive? Your child is likely to be the best source of advice about what they'd find helpful from you as a parent, but it's sometimes easiest for a child to discuss this in relation to a neutral set of examples, such as those below.

- ***Thank you for telling me this:*** remembering to say thank you is a big part of helping your child feel that they've done the right thing in sharing something with you. This will help develop their confidence in being honest about difficult situations.
- ***Would you like me to share my thoughts or just listen?*** Being ready to hold back on your own advice makes it easier for your child to feel they'll have as much space as they need to get their words out. It means they don't have to worry about being misunderstood and

it allows time for their feelings to settle before they think about what to do next.
- *Would you like a hug?* Love and compassion doesn't solve the situation but it bolsters the emotional energy reserves and it reminds your child that your first response is one of love, not blame. As discussed on p79, if a child isn't doing well at school, they often feel embarrassed or ashamed. Opening with love, not blame or disappointment, makes it easier for your child to be honest with you.
- *Maybe you could tell me a bit more about how you're feeling so that I can try to understand what's going on:* this response gently creates the opportunity for the teenager to practise the difficult process of putting feelings into words and it reminds your child that your first concern is to understand rather than direct.
- *What did you want to happen?* Teenagers often find themselves in situations that they did not intend: a child who doesn't get started with their homework until too late probably didn't mean this to happen. Acknowledging the difference between intention and outcome means that the child can show their better self as well as the situation where something has gone wrong. It also compassionately creates the space for a child to learn how to be more realistic when they make their plans; as later chapters will discuss, this will be a key skill for effective revision.
- *OK, well it sounds like this is a situation that doesn't have a quick fix: shall we think about how you're going to make it through? If you do get a detention, what happens then?* This response helps the child think about how they can manage the situation they're worried about; it's much more reassuring than implying that they've got to avoid the situation altogether. This will help your child learn how to develop a constructive outlook, even when they are feeling worried or stressed.
- *What do you think you should do now? Would you like me to offer some ideas?* This question starts to think about solutions, but it invites the child to speak first. This shows trust and respect; this will help

your child develop their ability to find solutions for themselves. It reminds the child that you're there to help and can offer ideas, but it avoids the demoralising implication that your ideas will be better than theirs. As a general rule of thumb, a child is much less likely to hear advice as criticism if they've asked for it first.

- ***What could you do differently next time? How can I support you in this?*** This question may need to be asked later on, after the immediate heat of the situation has passed. It focuses on what the child has done wrong, but it frames it constructively as an area for development in the future. Like the question above, it prioritises listening to the child's ideas first; this will develop your child's ability to use mistakes as a way to create positive changes. As above, you could ask if your child would like you to offer ideas; it will be easier for your child to listen to these if they had a choice about whether to hear them or not.

> **Y11 Student:** *It's really common for people to talk superficially about feeling stressed – people say that they are stressed about coursework or exams all the time. The standard response is, 'You'll be fine, you've got nothing to worry about' – this is from everyone. This isn't very helpful.*
>
> What do you think would help your child talk about their worries in a way that isn't superficial?
> What qualities are needed in the listener? Attentiveness? Patience? Compassion? Steadiness? Openness? Which of these are hardest to achieve?

I hope that the principles I've outlined in this chapter will help you embed patterns which will enable constructive conversations about school. These will help you understand your child's perspective, making it easier to see how to help them effectively.

In Part 3 I'll be offering guidance for how to help with the different scenarios that arise at different stages of the journey through school. One of the most likely areas for support at any age, however, will be the way your child studies when they are at home. Our next chapter, therefore, focuses on the general principles for this: if you want to help your child establish effective work habits, what should you do?

> **KEY IDEAS**
>
> - Children can find it difficult to talk about school with their parents, especially if something is going wrong.
> - It can be difficult for a teenager to explain how they are feeling and it can be hard for them to accept advice; this is partly because advice often feels like criticism.
> - When they are trying to talk about something difficult, teenagers need their parents to listen patiently and calmly.
> - Constructive conversations create enough space for emotions to settle before talking about next steps and they encourage the child to take a lead in thinking about what to do next.

CHAPTER 5

Establishing effective work habits

Y13 student: *I've never gone into an exam feeling like I've done enough.*

If you're flicking through this book, I wouldn't be surprised if you've headed straight for this chapter. Many students – and their parents – find it hard to be confident that their work habits are as they should be. This can be stressful for children and parents alike.

In this chapter, I'll be focusing on the everyday study routine centred around homework, not revision, and offering strategies which may be useful for any child, regardless of their age. I'm focusing on homework because your child will find it easier to revise effectively if their homework habits are good. In addition, revision advice depends on the nature of the exams your child is revising for and so I'll be coming to this in the age-specific chapters in Part 3.

It's worth being clear at the outset, though, that homework – or indeed revision later on – is likely to look very different from when you were at school. This is why I'll be encouraging you to take an interest in your child's thoughts about the types of study-habits that work for them, rather than fall into the trap of assuming that they should be studying in the same way you did. In addition, AI has already had a major impact on how teenagers work. Your child's school should provide guidance about which types of tech it's appropriate for your child to use for their homework. If a task is designed to be completed without access to AI, your child may need your support in creating a homework environment that removes the temptation of AI shortcuts.

Different work ethics

Broadly speaking, students tend to fall into one of the following three categories:

- **Significant disengagement:** you know there's a problem because the school's been in touch, telling you that effort levels are too low or there are gaps in homework or attendance. Perhaps the disengagement is because it's all become too much and your child is telling you they *can't do it* and it's become unbearable. Perhaps it's because your child seems entirely indifferent to outcomes and you're left with the frustrated feeling of *why don't they care about school?*
- **Seems to be going OK-ish, but should it be better?** Maybe it all sort of seems fine and you hear things like *good progress* from the school. But in the absence of superlative praise like *Excellent! Top of the class!* you're left with the thought that maybe it could all be a little bit more and your child isn't really fulfilling their potential.
- **Hyper-engaged, super-focused:** perhaps your child is pounding out their homework, everyone tells you how well they're doing and parents' evenings are full of comments like *I've got no concerns at all – the work is superb!* But you look at your child and can see the tiredness, the paleness, the tension and brittleness and you're left with a question mark in your head that won't go away, encapsulating the worry of *is it really supposed to look like this?*

If your child fits any of the descriptions above, this chapter will help you think about how to support them. If your child is disengaged, you'll find advice about how to motivate them to re-engage and work in a more reliable, steady manner. If your child is hyper-engaged, you'll find advice about how to help them set boundaries around their work so that it doesn't become overwhelming. If your child is in the middle category, you'll find advice that will help you and your child feel more confident about what working hard enough looks like day-to-day.

You'll find this advice centred around four key strategies, starting on p101. Before we get there, however, we need to explore some of the common misconceptions about what good work habits look like and how to achieve them.

Common misconceptions about motivation and work habits

Misconception #1: My child is disengaged and the problem is that they don't care enough about school.
One of the main misconceptions about motivation is that the essential ingredient is to care about the task. This misconception arises because at the top end of motivation there's evidently a connection: anyone who is working really hard will care a lot about what they are doing. There also appears to be a connection at the other end of the scale: if someone doesn't care at all, they probably won't put much effort in.

These two points of connection can obscure the fact that the correlation between caring and working hard isn't a neat, straight line. There are plenty of students in the disengaged category who are there because they care so much about getting something right that they've become functionally frozen through a fear of getting something wrong. Their procrastination or disengagement has arisen because they want to do well, they fear that they won't and it's so uncomfortable to risk it that the coping mechanism is to withdraw.

The misconception also arises because when a teenager has become really disengaged, they often say that they don't care. *I don't care* is a defence mechanism that shields a child from the pain of disappointing someone else's expectations: over time, saying *I don't care* can become so habitual a response that your child ends up really, genuinely believing that they no longer care about schoolwork. *I don't care*, however, is a statement that is rarely entirely true. It doesn't mean that your child wouldn't feel happier if they could meet, rather than disappoint, your expectations.

This means that if you want to motivate your child to re-engage, you may need to focus first on your own expectations. You need to have expectations that are straightforward for your child to meet because if you don't, you increase the risk that your child disengages. For your child to feel motivated to work, they need to know that they can reach the enabling, motivating place of looking you in the eye, hearing you say *well done, I'm proud of you* and knowing that you mean it. At its core, motivating your child to work harder centres around this: it needs to be safe for your child to drop their defensive shield and acknowledge that they *do* care about making you proud after all (see further, Chapter 1).

> **Student:** *Before I'd procrastinate, procrastinate – I never ended up getting much done. I was too busy giving myself an excuse not to work so that I wouldn't have to expose myself to the potential of failure. If you try, then you don't have any excuses if it doesn't go well. This is why I'd stop altogether. People assume that if someone isn't working, that means that they don't care. This isn't always true.*
>
> > Think about things your child has given up on: was it because they didn't want to do well or because they feared they wouldn't do well enough?

Misconception #2: If the marks could be better, I need to keep telling my child that they should be doing better so that they don't underachieve.
This one's tricky: as a teacher, my attention in the classroom is always focused on how to help students make progress. But I'm also aware of the damage it can do if *here's how to do better* gets warped into *you're not doing well enough now*. When a child believes that they're *not doing well enough now*, they feel that their efforts aren't generating the right return. If this continues, it can morph into the feeling that putting in the

effort is a waste of time; this can create a situation where motivation reduces.

Parents and teachers: the roles are different. Whatever the standard of your child's work, at school their teachers should be telling them – in every piece of feedback – how to improve it. At home, your role as a parent is different. Your child may need something to balance out the inevitably ever-present message at school of *here's how you can do better in the future.* At home, your child may need you to help them feel that there's good reason to be proud of their efforts today.

Misconception #3: If I remind my child that their results are important, this will motivate them to do well.
Your exams are important! Parents often try to motivate their children to work harder by telling them that they should care more about their exams and that the reward for their efforts will be *getting good grades.*

There are problems with this. For a start, it often doesn't work. If you're stuck in the head-banging loop of telling your child again and again that they need to *take school seriously*, you'll know this. Your child knows they're supposed to care about school; if this message hasn't already landed, repeating it again and again isn't going to get you anywhere.

What's more, caring about the work isn't actually necessary as an ingredient for making progress: if your child couldn't care less about *the really boring poems they've got to read for their English anthology*, that's not a disaster. They don't need to suddenly ignite a passion for English literature; what they need is to develop a pragmatic, transactional relationship with doing their homework.

The other problem with regularly reminding your child about the importance of their exams is that you risk increasing the stress levels in a way which impedes, rather than improves, their progress. There's going to be some degree of uncertainty about grade outcomes, whatever your child does. If the dominant reason for working is because the results really matter, there'll be an increase in the stress that arises from the fear of missing those grades (see further, Chapter 1). It's much more effective and reassuring to focus on something more controllable and dependable than the grade alone: this is why the advice in this chapter focuses on motivating the process, not the outcome.

> **Student:** *We had one English teacher – we all thought she was really strict, but she was better at helping us manage our stress. She gave me advice – she told me to control the controllables. I still remember this now.*
>
> - In the context of homework, what are the controllables?
> - How can you help your child focus on the things that are within their control, like sitting down to do it at a sensible time, putting their phone in a different room or contacting their teacher for advice if they couldn't complete it?

Misconception #4: I need to encourage my child to make as few mistakes as possible.
High standards are a good thing, but a problematic fear of mistakes isn't. It's easy to talk the talk of *mistakes help you learn*, but it's much harder to walk the walk. For a start, it's natural to be mistake-averse: no one enjoys getting something wrong. But I'd also argue that the current examination system has made it more likely that mistake-aversion develops into something more problematic.

There's a very long run-up to public exams (see further, Chapter 3). This means that there's a very prolonged focus on the importance of getting certain, very specific things right. For some students, the focus on not making a mistake in the exam can blur into the belief that it's important not to make mistakes at all.

This is problematic because it takes the success criteria for the end-point, final exam and assumes that they also apply to the learning process that builds up to this end point. In fact, the end-point exam and the learning process along the way are – educationally – two very different things. The exam is an assessment of what your child can do at the end of the course. It's a snapshot of knowledge and skills which already exist. The process of displaying knowledge and skills in an exam is very, very different from the process of learning this knowledge and building these skills during the course. As any teacher will tell you, the process of learning is bound to be full of mistakes. If a child is reluctant to make a mistake, they won't learn effectively, because at the moment where they most need to commit and *have a go*, they'll pull back. In the context of homework, fearing mistakes can make it much harder for a child to get started.

This means that, as a parent, you'll give your child a significant advantage if you can help them be calm and realistic about the inevitability of making mistakes. Your child needs to understand that mistakes are frustrating and often upsetting, but they're also an essential part of what drives learning forwards.

> **11–18 SENDCO:** *The fear of starting can be big: students are worried that if they're not performing to where they want to be or where other people expect them to be, then someone will judge that. Sometimes they get a bit stuck in thinking that they have to be a certain way or get a certain grade. This can be harder for kids with SEND, it's harder to think flexibly about different outcomes.*
>
> > Have there been times when fear about getting something wrong has made your child pull back from a task or activity?

Misconception #5: If my child really cares about doing well, then everything's fine.

The following statement is broadly true: *if my child cares, is motivated and works hard, they'll do well.* It's only *broadly* true, though, because the following statements are also true:

- a child can care, work hard and still end up with a lower grade than expected

- some children care so much about their grades that they experience problematic levels of stress at the prospect that their grades might not work out
- working hard has a tipping point: children who work too hard end up too tired to think effectively.

If your child is hyper-engaged and at risk of overworking or becoming too stressed about their exams, then their work habits are not constructive (see further, Introduction, p12). The strategies in this chapter will help you support your child in rethinking their relationship with schoolwork and setting boundaries which will help them establish a healthier balance in how they spend their time.

Misconception #6: They just need to make a plan and get organised.
Making a plan and *being organised* tend to be front-runners in standard advice about exam stress. There are good reasons for this: if a teenager has a plan and is organised, they'll feel more in control of the process and it'll be easier for them to use their time effectively.

The misconception, however, is the idea that they *just* need to get on with the planning. As Chapter 10 will discuss in more detail, making a revision plan is actually really difficult. It involves complex decisions, lots of moving parts and – crucially – making a plan means carrying the responsibility for the choices that the plan involves. This is why I'm focusing here on how you can support your child in developing a structured, planned relationship with homework. This will make it much easier for them to deal with the difficulties of revision planning when exams do roll into view.

A structured, planned relationship with homework: does that sound good? Is there a sigh of relief at the prospect that you might not need to nag or cajole your child into starting or stopping? I don't want to over-promise – no matter how good the work habits, don't expect a yogic-like calm every day of the week. The process of homework is rarely entirely predictable; there are bound to be some evenings where the plan buckles and has to adapt. But a *structured, planned relationship with homework* makes things much, much better, so let's think now about how to do this.

★ Key strategy #1: Finish lines

Ironically, conversations about motivation often focus on how to get started but the much more important question is where to stop. The stopping point sets the target, and if it's not sufficiently within reach, it's a rare child who will keep busting out efforts all the same.

When children are younger, the natural stopping point for a piece of homework is finishing the task. This is reasonably straightforward when homework tasks are short and designed to fit comfortably into the available time. As your child gets older, however, tasks become longer and more open-ended; this means that *finishing* homework can become harder to do. In addition, when it comes to revision, the finish lines become more complex: at KS3, teachers often set specific, boundaried revision tasks, but by the time your child is doing the final run-in to GCSEs, they'll be planning their revision themselves. If your child still believes they have to keep going until everything is 'finished', there's a risk that the to-do list becomes so overwhelming that they can't even get started.

This means that – perhaps counter-intuitively – as your child moves through secondary school, you may need to help them find a sustainable rhythm for homework that isn't only defined by *getting it all done.* You may need to help them decide clear starting points *and* clear finishing points that are not tied up with the quality or quantity of the work they are producing. Instead, you may need to help them set starting and finishing points that are defined by the time schedule of when they'll start and when they'll stop working, regardless of what the to-do list looks like.

> **Y12 Student:** *Telling yourself it's going to be done soon – this helps. You've gotta just do it.*
>
> Why is it easier to keep going when the finish line is clearly in view?
> Why is it harder to keep going when the finish line is far away?

★ Agreeing on a homework timetable

If you want your child to develop a *structured, planned relationship with homework*, they need to know what time they'll sit down to start their homework and what time they'll aim to stop. In effect, they need to decide a homework timetable that specifies which blocks of time on which days will be used for homework. Scheduling – and sticking to – a homework timetable has several benefits:

- it will be easier to support your child if there are fixed times when their phone goes away, and homework comes out
- it will be easier for your child to start working if they know – in advance – when they can stop
- our education system is built around time-capped exams: completing homework within set times will help your child develop their ability to get to the end of a task in the time available
- getting used to working at fixed times will help your child plan their revision schedule more effectively.

The younger your child is, the more their homework timetable will be directed by the school. At KS3, you'll probably receive information about what homework is set when and how long it should take; you can encourage your child to use this as the basis for drawing up their homework timetable at home. As your child gets older, they'll need to make more decisions about when and how long to work for: you'll find age-specific guidance for how to support them with this in the KS4 and KS5 chapters in Part 3 (see further, p177 and p214).

If your child is finding it difficult to get homework tasks finished in an appropriate amount of time, they may need guidance from their teachers about how to adapt their approach so that their homework fits within suitable time limits. A younger child may find it difficult to ask their teachers about this directly and they may need your support in contacting the school; as your child gets older, it's usually better to encourage them to initiate conversations with teachers themselves.

★ Is my child working hard enough?

If you are worried that your child isn't working hard enough, a clear homework schedule can help you – and your child – feel more confident that their efforts are suitable.

Should they be doing more? I'll be discussing this question in more detail in Chapter 10, but the headline answer is this: be wary of trying to answer this by wondering if your child's marks should be higher. It's much more constructive to think about whether the homework rhythm seems sustainable and steady for *today*. If your child has decided a daily schedule that they stick to reliably and which allows enough time for rest, hobbies and socialising too, then – if the school hasn't been in touch to tell you there are issues with attitude – your child is probably getting the balance about right. If you push your child to work harder in a way that is counterproductive for the balance of their day-to-day life, you're unlikely to end up with results which justify the guaranteed cost caused to their everyday rhythm.

★ Key strategy #2: Getting it done

The advice in Key strategy #1 included the idea that as children get older, they need to develop the skill of getting work done within a certain time frame. In effect, this means that they have to learn that **it's more important to *get something done* than it is to finish work to a certain standard.** This means that if – as a parent – you put too much emphasis on *getting it right,* you can inadvertently end up making it much, much harder for teenagers to work effectively at their homework.

If your child has just started secondary school, this principle may feel like a strange gear-shift from the way you supported your child with their homework in the past. When your child was at primary or junior school and learning basic numeracy and literacy, supporting them with *getting it right* was an important part of the process. This is because, educationally, primary or junior schools focus on building core, foundational knowledge. Children need to be accurate in this knowledge, and this is why – at that stage – it can be beneficial if parents notice and correct their child when they see a mistake. At secondary school, however, things are different. The reasons are as follows:

- **As a parent, it's much harder to know what 'right' should look like.** For foundational literacy and numeracy, the 'right' answer is clear. For a basic Maths sum like 2+2=4, a parent knows the answer as clearly as the teacher does. At secondary school, however, children are working towards public exams which are marked on very strict – sometimes surprising – criteria. Even if you did well at the subject yourself, your thoughts about how something should be done may not be in line with the rigidity of what the exam now requires. Even if you've dug out the mark schemes, you might know what the answer should look like by the end of the course, but during the interim stages, you won't know the full curriculum plans the teacher is using and where it's appropriate for work to be at x-point in time. As a parent, if you focus too much on whether your child's homework is 'right', there's a risk you – unintentionally – make your child believe their work is worse than it is and this is very unlikely to motivate them.
- **Caring too much about quality can impede productivity.** The single most important ingredient for progress is that a child keeps putting one foot in front of the other: if they're producing work –

regardless of quality – they'll be making progress. The problems come when they don't produce anything at all. If your child is too worried about whether their work is good enough, there's a risk they'll procrastinate or disengage.

The risk that *getting it right* can impede *getting it done* becomes more acute as children get older. As children grow up, their self-awareness and increasing maturity of thought means they're able to see the difference between what they do, what could be done and what others are doing. It's seeing these differences that means a child may start to feel uncomfortable about whether their work is good enough. A 5-year-old will draw a picture fairly freely; ask a 13-year-old to do the same task and they may be more hesitant. The 13-year-old will be much more sensitive to whether or not their drawing is as good as it should be.

Added to this is that as children get older, there's much more distance between the starting point for a new block of syllabus content and the finished product of what they'll do in the exam. Teachers often supply model answers to give students a view of what their work 'should' look like, but any student's first – or intermediate – attempts are likely to be some way short of this. This principle also applies to extended projects or coursework. Part of the difficulty many KS5 students experience in keeping up with coursework deadlines is because they feel their interim work isn't good enough; discomfort about producing work that doesn't seem *good enough yet* can mean that the student doesn't produce anything at all.

This means that all students need to be able to tolerate handing in work that is less good than they – or their teacher – would like it to be by the end of the process. All children need this, wherever they are on the attainment scale. Your role as a parent, therefore, is to remind your child that homework is about having a go; focusing on how to make it better is the domain of the teacher and the classroom. At home, the priority is to produce the work and then see what happens. This, more than anything, is the reason why, in the messaging that comes from a parent, **getting it done is more important than** *getting it right***.**

> **School Counsellor and Mental Health Lead:** *Young people need resilience; they need the capacity to take risks, to be able to handle making mistakes. I think there is just such a fear of getting it wrong, making mistakes, being judged for this. This can cause huge amounts of anxiety. This is in Y8/9. Then in Y10, Y11, when they get to exams it's the same fear of failure. Everything feels fear-laced.*
>
> In an exam, students should be carefully checking every detail; homework is different. What are the downsides of slowing down, checking details and worrying too much about mistakes during homework?

★ Key strategy #3: The cost:benefit ratio

As discussed earlier in this chapter, the child who isn't working hard enough day-to-day is unlikely to be motivated by the idea that the final exam grade will reward their efforts. For the vast majority of the school year, the exams are too far away for the reward to feel worth the cost of the effort *today*. Instead, the child who isn't working hard enough needs to find a cost:benefit relationship between effort and outcome that means it feels worth putting the effort in, right now, even if they'd much rather be doing something else.

The cost:benefit metaphor also matters for the child who is hyper-engaged. They need to learn to see more clearly where the cost of working too hard outweighs the benefit of getting that extra thing done.

★ Improving engagement

Rewards are family-specific: I wouldn't want the cost-benefit metaphor to imply that I'm suggesting cash payouts are the go-to option; in fact, I'd encourage you to think twice before paying your child in hard cash to do anything. *Do it and I'll get off your case* is often reward enough; sometimes holding back access to tech or similar generates enough motivation –

you can have your phone back when it's done. Often, all a child needs is to hear their parent say at the end, *I'm so pleased you did this – well done, I'm proud of you*.

I'm using a cost:benefit metaphor, however, because it highlights the idea that you'll need to think empathetically about the cost to your child first. You'll need to remember that doing homework does cost your child something: it takes up their time and energy; it means they can't do something else that they'd enjoy more; it also means they may have to open themselves up to the cost of writing down an answer, getting it wrong and feeling like their efforts were a *waste of their time*.

This means that if you want to work out how to incentivise your child effectively, you'll need to listen to your child's viewpoint first about the level of effort that they feel able to spend. If your child seems unmotivated, ask them what they can offer as a starting point for today. How long do they think they should sit down and study for? What time will they start and what time will they stop? What specific thing do they suggest they'll work on during this block of time? Tell them you want to support them by acknowledging the value of this effort; ask them what would help as an incentivising benefit or consequence.

Here's a caveat, though: if your child suggests an amount of work that is smaller than you're hoping, you're going to build a better route to increased engagement if you recognise its value all the same. Re-engaging is all about *deciding* and *delivering* and it's much better to support and praise your child on delivering what they've decided to do than it is to devalue their efforts by telling them *it's not enough*.

If your child has been very disengaged, once they start to re-engage it can be tempting to ask for more straightaway. Like any transactional deal, there's no harm in negotiating, but I'd encourage you to remember this: ask for too much and the deal will collapse. It's much better to get a steady rhythm sufficiently established first: once this is comfortably in place, it's much more likely that your child will find it easier to be more ambitious in what they think they can manage each evening and need fewer incentives from you to focus their mind on *getting it done*.

★ Reducing hyper-engagement

If your child is hyper-engaged, they'll be acutely aware of the benefits of hard work and worried about the potential costs of *not* working hard enough. Helping them understand the benefits of reducing their efforts can be more difficult.

If you are concerned that your child is working too hard, your child is likely to need reassurance from their teachers that it will – counter-intuitively – be more beneficial for them to reduce their efforts. It will feel much safer to your child to cut back their hours if their teachers are also telling them that this is sensible.

It's worth remembering how risky the change may feel to your child: if your child has been hard-working for years, they've already invested a huge amount into trying to do well. If they are nervous about compromising this by reducing their hours, you can help them by making the first step smaller and safer. *You're getting so tired: this won't help you do well, but I understand why this is a difficult change to make. So how about we try a different rhythm just for one or two weeks? Then we can take stock again. Let's experiment to see if the benefits of not being so tired turn out to be greater than the value of whatever it is you would have been working on instead.*

> **Y11 Student:** *It's hard to feel that you haven't been doing the right thing: you get praised for working hard so it's difficult to believe that working less hard might be better.*
>
> Are there examples you can share with your child from your own experiences which will reassure them that sometimes it's better to stop than to keep going?

★ Key strategy #4: Space to offload

As your child slogs through the long run-up to exams, it won't be surprising if they experience feelings of boredom, frustration or anger (see further, Chapter 3). These feelings need somewhere to go. If it's not possible for your child to voice them and know that their feelings are understood, the negativity of these feelings will sit in the mix, weighing the child down and in a way that makes it harder to work, not easier.

What's the worst bit about this homework? What are you most annoyed by? These types of questions let the heaviness come to the surface. As exams get closer, I tend to ask these questions more frequently when I'm working with teenagers who are hoping to improve their relationship with schoolwork. Often the frustrations relate to things that can't be changed because the syllabus and timeline is not up for debate; sometimes all I can say back to the child is *I'm not surprised you're feeling this way. If I could wave a magic wand and change things, I would.* Acknowledging the validity of the feelings may not seem to be offering much of a solution, but it's almost always the case that the student finds it easier to get on with the work – even if they really don't want to – if they've had the boost of some empathy first.

> **Student:** *I had a really good experience with another student, though. I told him how worried and how behind I felt. He said, 'Yes, the same, I'm so stressed, I never feel like I'm good enough, I feel behind.' This made such a difference because he didn't deny my feelings. I need to be heard.*
>
> If your child gets a chance to offload, how do they feel afterwards? Does this make them more or less ready to get on with their homework?

If you did flick straight through to this chapter, you weren't wrong: if the work habits at home are sound, things will probably be fine. But there is one more dimension to these work habits that we still need to discuss, and that's the language teenagers use to think about their schoolwork. And so the next chapter will focus on this: does your child think about their work in a way which is accurate, balanced and nuanced, or do they fall into blunt generalisations such as *there's **no** point, I **always** get it wrong* or *it's **never** OK to leave anything out*? And – if they do – how can you, as their parent, help them think about work in a way that is fairer, calmer, more constructive and more accurate?

> **KEY IDEAS**
> - An effective work rhythm at home needs clear starting and finishing points; agreeing a homework timetable will help to establish these.
> - If your child finds it difficult to finish their homework within the available time, they may need guidance from their teacher about how to adapt their approach.
> - For homework, it is much more important to focus on *getting it done* than *getting all of it right*.
> - If you think your child should be working harder, you will need to value and recognise their efforts day by day.
> - Teenagers may need space to vent frustrations or anger about their homework, especially in the run-up to exams.

CHAPTER 6

Building a balanced perspective

Student: *The thing that's changed for me now is the relationship with the guilt – I've finally learned that if I try, then whatever that looks like, that's fine.*

I wonder if the interview extract above is surprising? *If you try, that's all you can do*: surely this everyday message is so ubiquitous that it shouldn't take years and years for a student to develop a balanced relationship with how hard they should try and when they should – and shouldn't – feel at fault with how they've revised?

The truth is that developing a balanced perspective about exams can be surprisingly difficult because teenagers often think about exams in a simplified way. This chapter will outline some of the most common simplifications that may be there in the thought patterns. I'll also be explaining how you can help your child move to thoughts which are much more accurate, more realistic and more balanced.

Simplified thoughts

Simple rather than nuanced thoughts are partly a matter of brain development. A small child thinks in very simple, unnuanced ways because their brain is still developing: theirs is a world of *goodies* and *badies*, dogs who go *woof* and cats who go *miaow*. As they grow up, their thinking develops into something more complex and more nuanced. They gradually learn that dogs don't all sound the same and that things don't neatly fall into categories of *entirely good* or *entirely bad*.

Unfortunately, even when a brain has developed enough to facilitate nuanced, non-simplified thoughts, it's still much easier to think in a less nuanced way. In Chapter 2, I referred to Daniel Kahneman's Nobel Prize-winning research into thought patterns. His research identifies two modes of thinking: a quick, easy mode and a much more labour-intensive, intentional, slower mode.

The quick, easy mode is our default: it uses simplified thought patterns which are much easier to process. The slower mode is hard work; we have to choose to make use of it, but the effort involved means that often we don't want to go through the steps. The natural tendency is to revert back to simple generalisations, especially if someone is stressed, tired or upset.

Therefore, it's much quicker and easier for a teenager to think something generalised or exaggerated like *I'm going to fail* or *there's no point* or *I have to get my grades* than it is to go through the careful evaluation needed to produce a more accurate thought like *I know that I haven't revised photosynthesis as well as I wanted to, but I also know that that it'll probably only be 15% of the marks and there's a good chance I'll get some of these anyway because I can remember some of the things we did in class. I feel uncomfortable because I didn't revise in the way I planned, but – keeping it in perspective – I can see that it's probably not going to make more than 10% difference overall.*

Science Lead: *There's a dichotomy between you as a teacher saying don't worry it's only an end of topic test and you as a teacher saying pay attention, take this seriously, you need to know this.*

- Many teenagers feel they get mixed messages about school exams: does your child feel this way? Is it straightforward for them to maintain a balanced perspective, or is it easier to swing to the extremes of either *it's really important* or *I don't care about it at all*?

Commonly occurring simplified thought patterns

You're bound to hear your child talk in simplified or exaggerated generalisations. Some of these will refer to social dynamics, such as *she's always so mean*. Some might refer to your parenting style, for example, *you **never** listen to what I'm saying – why do you always make such a big deal of **everything**?* There'll also be plenty of generalisations that refer to how schoolwork is going. I'm going to discuss four of the most common of these now. Then on p118, I'll be outlining techniques you can use to help your child move past these generalisations into something more nuanced.

Simplified thought pattern #1: If I don't get my grades, it's all my fault.
This simplification happens because it's natural to take one statement and blur it with a seemingly equivalent opposite statement: *if you work hard, you'll make good progress* can get blurred with the idea that *if you don't do well, it's your fault for not trying hard enough*. The problem is that the first statement is substantially more true than the second. Equating these two statements ignores all the variables of external factors that are beyond our control. It mistakenly assumes that the only causal factor for an outcome is effort.

In over 20 years in the classroom, I have never, ever, once made a set of predictions that matched the final outcomes perfectly and this isn't because I don't know the kids, haven't marked enough work or I don't understand the exam requirements. Predictions don't always match results because grade outcomes in any one subject are impacted by a whole load of external factors beyond any one person's control: maybe the exam timetable throws a curveball and the paper which would normally have scored the best marks is scheduled right at the end of the most intense three days in the process; maybe the student gets ill and finds it hard to concentrate; maybe the exam marker was off point; maybe the student gets lucky and the stuff they happened to look at just before the exam comes up and gives them a boost which tips their score upwards.

I don't think anyone would dispute the fact that grade outcomes are a mixture of factors your child can control – such as how they revise – and factors they can't do much about. The problem is, however, that it's easy for a teenager to lose sight of the interplay between these different factors. Teenagers hear motivational messages about *working hard* on such a regular basis that the familiarity of this message can generate a simplified thought that grade outcomes are entirely down to their efforts.

The other reason why the simplification happens is because students have to plan their revision before they know what the exam questions will be, but they assess their revision retrospectively after they've seen the paper. Hindsight offers a clear view on what would have been the optimal way to revise, but it's a view that isn't fair. It often ignores the fact that these decisions were much harder to make when the question paper wasn't known.

For public exams, the risk increases that a teenager forgets the uncertain context within which revision decisions had to be made. There's a time gap of months between revising and finding out the results: this makes it much more likely that a teenager will retrospectively feel at fault when the grades are in, feeling cross about what they think they should have done differently.

> **Y12 Student:** *When the results were coming, I couldn't stop thinking about it, couldn't sleep. I started questioning if I'd done enough revision – I didn't know if I should have pushed myself further. There was that doubt that I hadn't put in enough effort.*
>
> > How does your child respond when they get a disappointing mark? Does your child immediately start thinking about what they should have done differently? Are they retrospectively cross with how they worked?

Simplified thought pattern #2: There's no point – I'm going to fail anyway.
Pass / fail: these are clear, simple categories. It's much easier to think about outcomes in this simplified way than it is to pause and evaluate exactly how many marks might be generated by 30 minutes of revision on a Wednesday evening. It's particularly difficult if the child is used to thinking that the point of revision is to pass the exam: 30 minutes of revision probably isn't going to dramatically shift an outcome. If its value is assessed as whether or not it's going to flip the *pass / fail* switch, it's unsurprising if any individual burst of revision seems fairly pointless.

The problem is, of course, that the thing that does flip the *pass / fail* switch is a series of revision sessions; to feel motivated about doing each small bit of revision, the child needs to see the benefit of that small bit. This means that they need to break out from the ungranulated, simplified *pass / fail* mode of thinking. This is one of the reasons why the advice on motivation in Chapter 5 focused on creating a value/reward system based on individual, small pieces of work, rather than by reference to the final, big, ungranulated grade.

Simplified thought pattern #3: I don't know what to do next.
Secondary school involves lots of decisions: how hard to work, which subjects to take, what career path to follow. Decision-making is also at the centre of effective revision planning. The age-specific advice in later chapters will focus on the specifics of these different types of decision, but underpinning each one is the risk that a simplified, unnuanced thought gets in the way: *But what if this isn't the best decision? What happens if this option isn't good enough because there's something out there which might be better?*

Best is a simplified category: it ignores the nuanced reality that it's almost impossible to feel sure that any individual decision offers the *best* way to achieve future goals and step smoothly through all the unknown variables along the way. It also ignores two important truths:

- The margin between one set of decisions and another is often much smaller than the absolute categories of *best* v. *not-best* suggest.

- Getting better at making decisions is an iterative process: teenagers need to learn to make a decision, get on with it, and then review and adapt as necessary. Chasing the *best* decision ignores the fact that it's more important to get some sort of plan in place, get started and then review it as the process evolves.

Decision-making becomes much harder if it's centered around the question of *is this decision the best one*? Any decision will have its downsides; as soon as the downsides appear, it can feel to the student like there might be another, *better* option out there. Trying to find the *best* decision can mean that students end up prevaricating, flipping from one option to another – wasting time and energy along the way. When students get stuck in the uneasy feeling that their decision might not be quite right, procrastination sets in and it's harder to make any progress at all.

> **Student:** *Sometimes I'm overwhelmed by the amount of options there are.*
>
> Will it help your child if decisions feel too complicated?

Simplified thought pattern #4: I have to get my grades.
One of the simplifications which happens frequently within our thought processes is that we often blur *want* with *need*. This blurring happens partly because we usually do want the things that we need; it also happens because, when it comes to things like grade outcomes and life choices, *need* is a very complex category, full of complicated evaluations about pros and cons of things that are far away in the future. It's much easier to focus instead on what feels preferable.

Your child might want to get particular grades for a sixth form or post-school option; they might really, really want to get these grades for all sorts of valid, understandable reasons. They might want these grades so much that it *feels* like they need them. But this is a very different thing from actually *needing* to get those grades: *need* implies that life falls apart if the grades don't land. *Need* implies that nothing else will do.

The problem with blurring *want* with *need* is that it's easy to start talking about grade outcomes as if they are *necessary* rather than *preferable*. Language such as *I've got to get my grades* creeps into the thought patterns: inevitably, once *want* gets reframed as *need*, the pressure increases. If grades start to seem *necessary*, the cost of missing those grades ratchets up and so too does the exam stress.

> **Child and Adolescent Psychotherapist:** *As a child and adolescent psychotherapist, I see the teenagers who are struggling the most with their anxiety. I'm thinking of two Y13s. They can't eat. They are making themselves ill. They are so full of what-ifs: 'What if my mind goes blank, what if this one thing comes up that I don't know?' It's as if there's no future other than the exact one they've planned out. There's no flexibility. It's really helpful to be able to talk through possible outcomes. I did an exercise today with a young person talking through the what-ifs; it was all survivable but teenagers need help to get to a place where they know that it is survivable.*
>
> Thinking through the *what-ifs* makes it easier for a teenager to separate *want* from *need*. Will it be easier for your child to feel calmer about their exams if they've thought in advance about how they'll handle it even if something does go wrong?

★ Techniques to help build a balanced perspective

Technique #1: Balance out the soundbites

The first way that parents can help their children build a balanced perspective is to be aware of the types of simplified soundbites that close down a more nuanced way of thinking. The table below sets out pairs of messages. The left-hand column includes things that your child is likely to hear regularly. The right-hand column contains a counterbalance which you can say to your child to help them build a more balanced perspective.

Simple soundbite	A more balanced perspective
Your exams matter!	Different things matter at different times in your life: your exams are important right now, but their importance will change over time.
You can make your dreams come true if you work hard enough!	Hard work is important but luck also plays a role: sometimes the wind blows in our favour, sometimes it doesn't.
If you work hard, you'll be fine!	Working hard puts you in a good position, but external factors play a role too. If you work hard but don't get the grades, it's not necessarily your fault.
Find the revision method that's best for you!	There will be pros and cons for different approaches, but the differences between them will be less than you think. Overthinking it will take time and energy which could be better used getting on with the revision.
It'll be great if you get your grades!	I understand how disappointing it'll be if you don't get the grades, but disappointment is different from disaster. There'll be a route through either way.

I should have revised differently.	Hindsight makes this decision seem simpler than it was at the time. If you'd made a different decision, the paper might have been different. 'Could' doesn't always mean that you 'should' have done things differently. Use this experience to face forwards; you can't change the past.
Don't worry – it'll be fine!	It's natural to be worried when an outcome feels uncertain, but this doesn't mean that it's going to go badly. Don't lose sight of the different ways I'm here to support you: I want to help you do well, but I'll also be there to help you if something surprising happens.
Just do your best!	You can't absolutely guarantee the outcome, all you can do is put in a reasonable, sensible amount of effort. If you like, we can talk this through so that it's easier for you to know when you've tried hard enough.
I only want you to be happy!	I hope you'll have a life that – overall – feels meaningful and fulfilling, but it'll have its ups and downs all the same. No one is happy all the time.

Y10 Student: *GCSEs are often an example teachers use for something very important – if teachers are the only source of advice, you can end up thinking exams are more important than they are.*

Teachers have to focus on the importance of exams: that's their job. Parents can take a broader perspective – what are the things you can tell your child that they may not hear at school? Is there anything you'd add to the table above?

> **11–18 Inclusion Lead:** *If we all talked more about the fact that worry is natural, this would help. We need to help pupils build this resilience so that they can manage this feeling: we can tell them that it's natural to feel like this, but here's what to do if it gets too much.*
>
> - Does it help to be told *not to worry*?
> - Is it more useful to take a more nuanced perspective and learn how to understand and handle this feeling?

★ Technique #2: Using a score out of ten

Evaluative thinking is the process that allows us to break free from the simplified idea that something is either entirely one thing or entirely not: it does this by thinking about scores on a more granulated scale. If you think that your child is getting something out of perspective, it's worth asking them to *give it a score out of ten* so that they can learn to view it in a more nuanced way.

Here are some examples of how you can help your child do this. I've tied them to things you might hear your child say, but the technique can be adapted for any sort of simplified, absolute statement.

There's no point revising – I'm going to fail.

- *Give me an example of one piece of revision you could do right now. Give it a score out of ten. 0/10 means that it has absolutely no value at all. 10/10 means that it'll transform your test score. What value do you think it would have? Does it have absolutely no point at all or does it have some point? If it's got some point, then let's think about why it's worth doing now.*

It'll be my fault if I fail.

- *You're right that your efforts play a part in the outcome, but what about the other things that have an impact too, such as how hard the test is or subjective decisions in the way it's marked? Let's write a list of some of these and score each out of 10. How much does each of them matter?*

I have to get my grades.
- *You're blurring how much you want these grades with how much you need these grades. Let's separate these out. How much do you want the grades – what's the score out of 10? Then let's think about how much you need the grades: think of something that you definitely need more and something you definitely need less. What scores would you give to each of these and why?*

★ Technique #3: Which option is better?

It's much easier to choose between two options than it is to feel sure that any individual choice is the best one possible. If your child finds it hard to make decisions, you can help them by reminding them that there is no such thing as a single, ideal thing to do next. Any decision will have pros and cons: rather than chasing the *best* thing to do next, it's much more constructive to settle on an option that seems *better* than something else.

Set out below is a sample structure you can use to help your child focus on *which option is better – this one or that one?* I've structured it around revision or homework decisions. The sample structure is designed for a child who isn't sure about which piece of work to do next, but you could adapt the framework for other decisions such as choosing GCSE or A level options or working out how many hours of revision to do at the weekend. It sets out the questions you can ask your child to help them focus on deciding between two possible options, rather than worrying about whether it's the *best* plan.

- *There's no one way to get this done: if you're getting stuck on chasing the best option, you'll be wasting time and effort. It's much more constructive to get on with something. Once you've made one decision, you can review it afterwards and adapt your plans as you go. Decision-making gets easier with practice.*
- *Can you give me two examples of a piece of work you could do right now? What are the pros and cons of each one?*
- *Now can you tell me which one is the better option and why?*

- *It's counterproductive to get too stuck on the decision-making: if this option seems better than that one, then it's got value. So how about you get started with that? Then we can repeat the process once you've got this first thing finished.*

Once your child has explained their reasons and worked out which of the two options is better, imagine that this is what they hear next: *That sounds sensible; you've got good reasons for doing this – I want you to know I support this decision whether or not you get the outcome you're hoping for.* Think how much easier it'd be for your child to decide what to do next if they know you approve of their actions, regardless of outcome.

> **Student:** *You don't know if your revision will be enough until August. Then there's the fear of when I get my results – am I going to be angry about the two hours where I switched off my laptop and I could have been working instead. Am I going to be angry with my past self?*
>
> - Does your child worry about whether their decisions are the right ones?
> - Would it help them to hear that they can't be expected to do more than make the decision that seems reasonably sensible at the time?

★ Technique #4: Thinking through the *what-ifs...*

This technique is designed to help your child manage the *what-ifs* of something going wrong. I've exemplified it by using GCSE or A level grades as the framework, but it can be applied to any situation where your child is worried about an outcome.

I've used grade outcomes as the frame for this technique because teenagers often feel anxious about the very specific consequences connected with these, like entry to a particular sixth form, university or training programme. Thinking through the *what-ifs* will help your child think in a more balanced way about getting – or missing – the grades for their preferred next course. It avoids the imbalance of preparing in a way which focuses only on success. There are two ways to balance out the thinking:

1. **Pros *and* cons of both**: it's much healthier to think about upsides *and* downsides of getting or missing the grades. If your child mentions how much they want one particular outcome, it's helpful as a parent to encourage them to keep alternatives in mind: *Yes, it'd be great, that's why it's Plan A, but would there be any downsides? What are the pros and cons of Plan B? I know you much prefer one to the other, but it's useful to stay as measured as you can about each.*
2. **What happens if you don't get the grades?** It's much easier for a child to know what they'll do if a test or exam goes well. It's a pleasant thing to think about and your child will probably already know what they'll do if the outcome is as hoped. The alternative outcome often feels much hazier because it's uncomfortable to think about. *What would you do if the exam doesn't go well? How could I support you then?* These questions help a child begin to think it through; if they're younger and it's a low-stakes test, it'll help them remember that there are lots of second chances ahead. If they're older and the consequences are bigger, it will take the sting out of the shock of the disappointment if they've already got a sense of what their next step could be.

When I do workshops for parents, I often hear the worry that offering to support when the grades go wrong might make it too easy for a child to slack off in their efforts. If this is something that troubles you too, I'd encourage you to go back to the material in Chapter 5: usually children want to do well. They stop trying when it becomes too difficult or too risky to keep investing their efforts in something where there's too high a likelihood of disappointment. A child is much *more* likely to stay engaged if they know that their parent understands the cost of the efforts and is ready to support them if something goes wrong.

> **Student:** *The advice I'd give to my Y12 self, now that I'm at university? I'd say whatever happens it will turn out OK – maybe you'll get into your first choice, maybe you won't but whatever happens, then a little bit along the line you'll be happy with that.*
>
> • This student gives the advice that things usually turn out OK in the end. This advice is easier to give retrospectively than it is to believe at the time: why is this?

★ A balanced preparation for results day

Did you buy this book because you want to help your child get good grades? Or did you buy it so that you could think about how to support them even if they don't?

It's an important pair of questions. Perhaps you're thinking, *yes to both!* I hope so, but it wouldn't be surprising if the first *yes* was more obviously present when you started reading. We're parents: we want things to go well for our children. But, during the long run-up to public exams, children have to carry the uncertainty that they don't *know* if it's all going to be OK. They need support from us, as their parents, for both sides of the coin (see further, Chapter 1).

I'm writing this book because imprinted in my memory are the faces of the teenagers who weren't able to tolerate the risk that their exams might not be OK. They couldn't trust that they'd find a way through *whatever* happened on the day. I can still see the students who I watched getting angrier or more absent or thinner or paler or somehow smaller and more brittle. I see their faces even now because I still wish I had been able to help them better so that they left school older, bigger, stronger, and more at ease with themselves than when they started, whether or not their exam grades were as they wanted. I feel so sad about what the exam experience did to them.

So let's take the *it's-all-fine* picture of smiling children clutching gleaming results out of view for the moment. Let's look at the other side of it. Let's imagine the scenario where your child opens up their envelope and you see their face fall. But let's imagine that, in this scenario, what happens next is as follows. Let's imagine that these thoughts are ready to surface in your child's mind: *Yeah, I'm gutted. But I know that this disappointment will fade. I know that I made considered decisions about how to work; I set the boundaries that I needed to maintain a constructive work rhythm and a healthy balance. I know that I did my reasonable best. I know that life is full of twists and turns but that if I stay steady and thoughtful, it'll probably work out in the long run. I know that I won't always deliver what someone else wants and I understand that their expectations don't have to be what defines me. I know all this but can we go home now because I'd still like a hug and the privacy to cry for a bit. I think I'll feel better if we do this; I'm glad that you're here for me in the moments that don't go to plan. I think I just need to pause for today and then tomorrow, let's start afresh.*

Imagine that. Think of this scenario side by side with the *you've-aced-it-well-done* first image. If I had a wishing-well, I'd wish that your child gets the all-smiles, let's-celebrate version of results day. I hope that this book will help you to help them to get there. But if you can see in the second scenario something equally valuable because it evidences the presence of dispositions which will keep your child confident, motivated and resilient far into the future, then keep reading. It's time to get specific about what your child may need during each stage of the secondary school journey. Let's move on to Part 3.

KEY IDEAS

- Children often think in a simplified way; this can lead to conclusions which are inaccurate.
- You can help your child learn how to think in a more balanced, accurate and realistic way about how hard to work, what to do next and how to respond to their exam results.
- Useful techniques for this include balancing out simple soundbites, using evaluative thinking, aiming for the *better* rather than the *best* decision, and thinking through the *what-ifs*.
- As a parent, you can support your child in a balanced way if you think about how to help them do well *and* how to help them manage a situation where they feel disappointed by their grades.

PART

Age-specific advice

Part 3 offers age-specific advice; this is so you can find the material that is most relevant to your child. The journey through school, however, is a sequence. If your child is in the sixth form, their experience will have been shaped by what happened at KS4 and KS3. This means there may be material in earlier chapters which helps you make sense of something that is happening now; equally, if your child is in KS3, you may find it useful to read ahead into the later chapters to build your understanding of what's likely to come next.

A REMINDER ABOUT LABELS

- **KS3** refers to Key Stage 3, i.e. Years 7–9
- **KS4** refers to Key Stage 4, i.e. Years 10–11
- **KS5** refers to Key Stage 5, i.e. Years 12–13

CHAPTER 7

Getting started at secondary school

Senior Deputy Head: *At its worst, I've seen students who can't walk into an exam room because they are experiencing debilitating panic attacks and are lying collapsed on the floor.*

I don't mean to frighten you with what you've just read above: most teenagers don't end up with exceptional exam stress. But for those who do, the beginnings started long before they tried to step into that exam room. This means that it's worth thinking about how the experience at KS3 shapes the mindset that teenagers take with them into GCSE and beyond.

Spoiler alert, though: this chapter isn't really about exams. It's about the process of learning that takes place in Years 7–9 and how to help your child adapt to secondary school in a way that prepares them for later success.

What's different about secondary school?

Starting secondary school means launching into a whole new type of experience. Secondary schools are bigger, busier and more complicated than primary or junior schools. Your child will need to navigate more subjects, more teachers, more classrooms, more clubs, more people.

There'll also be quite a lot more mess. Schools often try to tidy things up before parents visit, so you might not see the mess in all its glory, but it's there all the same. Forgotten jumpers on benches, piles of exercise books in classrooms, trainers or sports bags hanging out of half-open lockers: it's often the case that secondary schools are quite literally much messier than primary schools. I mention the mess because it's a very real symbol of the metaphorically messy experience your child will need to adapt to.

Everyone is dashing from here to there, doing multiple things. The same classroom is used by different teachers for form time and subject teaching. The piles of paper in the corner might belong to the PSHE team, or the French department, or maybe there are some History resources mixed in as well which a cover teacher left behind by mistake. Whoever has been tasked to tidy the room up probably does care about making it smarter, but they're also thinking about their Y11 lesson plans or the admin for a school trip that they're running, or their inbox is bulging with emails, or they've got to pause everything because a child is in tears and needs help *now*.

More subjects, more teachers, more classrooms, more clubs, more people: this all combines into an experience that is energising, stimulating, educationally enabling, but it is also complex and messy. It's full of different commitments and different expectations and different people asking different things at different times and that's a lot to get used to.

Why exam marks shouldn't be your main focus at KS3

When parents are trying to work out if it's all going OK for their child, the natural thing to look at are the marks from KS3 assessments. On the surface, exam percentages seem to offer a moment of tidied-up, neatly labelled clarity. *Here's how you're doing in English*: 72%. Or at least it looks like clarity.

At KS3, this sort of label appears clear, but in practice it isn't. 72% is clearly better than 71%, clearly less good than 73%, but it's got to be understood in the messy context of KS3. Your child – and you – both have to run it through the question of *is it going OK and if not what do we do about it?* That's a question which can't be answered without factoring in complicated, messy things like aptitude, age, attitude, aspiration, class averages and – unless it's a mark like 98% – it's a question which more often than not throws up the extremely messy answer of *well, maybe OK, but could it and should it be better?*

This means that if you want to support your child effectively at the start of secondary school, as a parent you need to give limited attention to the marks because – to be blunt – they won't get you very far. If there's a genuine issue, the school should tell you about it anyway. Instead, you need to start thinking about the mess and what it takes to thrive within it.

> **Assistant Head, Teaching & Learning** *The parents are very anxious right from the start about where their child sits in the pack.*
>
> - When school reports come home, what do you look at first? Exam marks or attitude grades? What does your child look at first?
> - Are you worried about whether your child is doing better or worse than others in their class, or do you focus on how happy and motivated they seem in themselves?

Talking with your child about school

If you're going to help your child adapt to secondary school, you're going to need them to tell you about it. This isn't always easy, though: *How was your day? Fine.* You might be blessed with very chatty children who tell you all sorts about what happened that day, but if – like most parents – you get a monosyllabic response to the *how-was-your-day* question, it's worth pausing to think about why. There are two main barriers – let's look at them now.

Barrier #1: Talking can be tiring

At school, children are *on* (see further, Chapter 3). Sometimes, when they get home they want to be *off* and say nothing at all. Most kids don't want to talk the minute they walk through the door and they also don't want to talk if they're doing something else. Interrupt them while they're doing their homework or watching TV and you probably won't get much.

The best timing for a conversation tends to be after your child has had a chance to unwind and re-energise. It's also much easier for a child to talk if they are not doing something else that demands their attention. Talking in parallel to everyday, routine events such as mealtimes or during chores or short car journeys doesn't get in the way of anything else and this makes it much easier to do. It also has reassuring boundaries: the meal will end, the car journey will stop: it's much easier for a child to find the energy for a conversation if they know it's not going to go on and on.

I say *not doing something else* but this rests on the assumption that their phone isn't in their hand. It's in every child's interests for there to be times when their phone is out of sight, out of mind and I'd say that this becomes increasingly true as they get older. When you're thinking about the times when the phone goes into a drawer in Y7–9, it's worth factoring in the types of time it'd be useful to leave free for conversation and the opportunities you'll lose if your child has their phone out during short-ish car journeys or at the table.

Barrier #2: How was your day?

How was your day? It's worth noticing that – for a KS3 student – this question is difficult to answer. It's an evaluative question that asks your child whether things went well or not. But remember, their day will have been messy: some bits will have gone better than others, there will have been multiple moments that felt *OK* or *not really* and for lots of different reasons.

So, my advice is that the *how-was-your-day* question isn't really the best opener. It doesn't do any harm to ask it – after all, it's a standard part of friendly interactions – but don't be surprised if it doesn't yield much fruit. Let's think now about which questions would be better and why.

★ Questions that will help your child

As a child matures, their brain develops: this means they can move beyond simple thoughts into something more complex (see further, Chapter 6). Like any other aspect of child development, however, there isn't a one-size-fits-all timeline for this. When your child moves from the *here's your peg* simplicity of primary or junior school to the *French is in classroom R02* complexity of secondary school, their brain may or may not be ready for the degree of difference that they have to navigate in one and the same day. On a Tuesday, they might have five different teachers, five different sets of expectations: even in the schools that really strive for consistency, one teacher will care more about an underlined title than another.

You might be surprised if I tell you that by the end of the school year, a large number of Y7 children still don't know their timetable; they might not even know their teachers' names. Surprising, perhaps, but true and probably more common than you might expect. It's something that happens in Y8 and even Y9 as well. When KS3 students don't know their timetable or they can't remember what they need for each day, they end up getting in trouble: they turn up to lessons without the right books or they forget to do their homework on the right day. This makes it harder for them to learn effectively.

Your child may need considerable help in getting their head round the practicalities of the school day. There's no need to pack their bags for them – in fact, it's counterproductive if you do – but you'll do them a big favour if you regularly ask them about what they'll need for school and why. Your child will also need to interact with a wider range of people now they are at secondary school: this means navigating different reactions, values and expectations. Discussing these with your child can be transformative in helping your child feel more comfortable in this new, complex environment. It will also help your child develop their ability to think in a way that is nuanced (see further, Chapter 6).

★ Examples of better questions to ask your child

The most useful questions, therefore, that you can ask your child at the start of secondary school have nothing to do with *how is it going* and everything to do with *is this new complexity seen and understood?*

Set out below are the types of questions that help your child do this. There's an explanation with each one to highlight why it is more useful and easier to answer than *how was your day?* The questions are examples – they're not designed to be asked all at once. They are suggestions of the sorts of things it's helpful to have up your sleeve for those times when your child is ready and able to talk.

- ***What lessons did you have today?*** This is a great opener; it gives you an instant foothold to ask more – *Maths! Just like yesterday! Were you doing the same thing or something different?* Every time your child tells you something about *what* they have done, you are actively helping them learn: re-verbalising lesson content makes it more likely they'll remember it for longer, making it easier for them to do well in the next lesson.
- ***Did they set any homework?*** Finding out about homework helps your child remember what they need to do that evening. It also creates the opportunity to go a bit deeper: *Why do you think this has been set? What does it help you learn?* Questions like these help your child think about the value of different types of tasks; over time, this will help them plan independent study – such as revision – more effectively.
- ***Oh, you had French – can you remind me the name of your French teacher?*** This is a route to talking more about what lessons are like. *Does she set lots of written work? Does she call on you to answer individually? Is this similar or different to other teachers?* Questions like this will help your child think about the different ways to

learn and this will help them make better decisions when they need to study independently.

- **Which teacher was the strictest today?** Noticing and discussing which teachers care about what will help your child feel clearer about different types of expectations. It also lays important groundwork for the moments when your child may need to tell you about something that went wrong for them. Talking in a kind and compassionate way about classroom dynamics will help your child trust that your reaction will be fair and empathetic. *So, your friend got sent out of the lesson today? What do you think about this? Do you understand why the teacher did it? How do you think your friend felt about it?* Conversations like these will make it much easier for your child to reflect constructively about their experience if something similar happens to them.

- **Did you have assembly? What was the message today?** Values tend to be expressed in short, simple taglines, such as *excellence, ambition, resilience*, and they are often exemplified by something attention-grabbing or exceptional. You can help your child develop a nuanced, realistic understanding by thinking about how they apply to ordinary, everyday life. *So you were talking about resilience today? That's great – what examples did they use? What do you think resilience might look like day-to-day for you?*

- **Who did you chat to at lunch? Were they in a good mood?** As your child moves through adolescence, their friends will sometimes be unhappy, sometimes for very difficult reasons. Creating regular opportunities for your child to tell you if someone they know is sad will make it much easier for them to open up about their own feelings too. In addition, teenagers often feel very responsible for how their friends are feeling: creating regular opportunities to talk about this will reduce the risk that your child takes on a greater level of responsibility for someone else's happiness than is appropriate at that age.

> **11–18 Inclusion Lead:** *Emotional resilience work needs to be there; students need these skills from KS2 onward. We can do this by talking about things that go wrong or talking about how they feel about things, about tests. If we did this at KS2 and KS3, they'd have the resilience in place to help them with KS4.*
>
> Which does your child find easier: talking about their own feelings or discussing how other people reacted to something?
> Will thinking about other people's reactions help your child to understand their own feelings better as well?

★ Reducing the complexity of KS3: Smartphones

It's worth being clear that the messiest, most complicated, hardest-to-wrap-your-head-around area of life at KS3 will almost certainly play out in the mind-scrunching world of smartphones. Group chats, social media judgements, momentary responses that take on an indelible digital footprint: online everything moves faster, shouts louder, is more chaotic and extreme.

What are you going to say about smartphones? In the early discussions that shaped this book, I got asked this a lot. It's a tricky one – not least because things change quickly and by the time you're reading this, decisions about smartphones in schools and access to social media at a young age may already look quite different. It's also tricky because social media is exactly what its label suggests: it is the medium for socialising. If you're worried about potential harms to your child, social isolation is one of the most toxic. If everyone else has a smartphone, it's really hard for an individual child to be the one who's left out.

But I would say this and I'll say it as loudly and clearly as I can: **if your child has a smartphone, please think very seriously about the number of hours they have access to it.** Please strike a balance between the fun and relaxation that technology can provide and the number of hours in the day where your child might end up deep in the mess. I'd urge you to put firm boundaries around life in the online world and make sure that it doesn't impinge on sleep and well-being. These boundaries will help reduce the risk that tech sucks your child away from access to calmer, steadier modes of being where less is going on and everything is easier to process. Please make sure that they're not so busy messaging and talking to others online that there's no bandwidth left for talking to you.

> **Student:** *I think social media does impact how much time you have, how busy you are. It's kind of fine while everything's fine in terms of friends and stuff – then it's positive, it's a way you can relax. As soon as problems begin, then the problems come home with you, there's no escape from it.*
>
> How can you help your child make sure that at home there's a chance to step away from the complexity of what's happening at school?

★ A KS3 checklist: Is it going ok?

If you ask your child the types of questions exemplified on p133, you'll get a good sense of how well they are coping with the complexity of secondary school. You can use the checklist on p137 to help you work out whether your child is comfortably managing the complexity of KS3 or whether it's too much for them to get their head around.

1. Does my child know their timetable and the names of their teachers?
2. Can my child remember something about what they did in at least a couple of lessons that day?
3. Can my child talk about what other people in their year are doing?
4. Does my child understand behaviour expectations and are they starting to understand why different people expect different things?
5. Can my child verbalise the school's values? Do they have their own view on when and why these values are important? Can they think about the nuances behind the simple taglines?
6. Does my child know what their homework is and – if they're sitting down in a room without distractions from their phone or similar – do they have a daily rhythm where they get on with it and get the majority of it done?
7. Is my child cheerful and enthusiastic in general? Do they seem – on the whole – to be energised and open to new experiences? Do they seem happy and well in themselves?
8. When my child is sad, do they seem open to talking about this?

If the answer is broadly *yes* to most of these questions, then it's very likely indeed that at the very least it's going *OK-enough*. At KS3 – with all of the variables of development coming up the pipeline – going *OK-enough* is probably all that you need.

I'm encouraging you to focus on *OK-enough* rather than *as-good-as-it-possibly-could-be* because it's much better at this age for a child to feel like there's a broad margin of tolerance for what counts as OK. If you narrow the margin with too sharp a focus on hitting specific standards, you'll make it much more likely that your child ends up fearing that it's all going to go wrong. Fearing it's all going to go wrong is one of the main impediments to making good progress (see further, Chapter 5).

> **School Counselling and Mental Health Lead:** The 'you'll end up working for a fast-food restaurant' idea comes up shockingly often, but there's a huge margin between getting all 9s and working for a fast-food restaurant. I don't know why the only two possibilities seem to be total success or no success at all.
>
> - What's your margin of tolerance for *going OK*? Have you started to encourage your child to aim for very specific outcomes or do you encourage them to remember that there are lots of different ways to lead a happy and fulfilled life?

But isn't *OK-enough* too low a bar?

I'm conscious that it may sound un-aspirational to suggest that *OK-enough* is all that's needed at KS3. Maybe you're thinking something like this: *School should be about maximising potential! If they're finding things easy, they should be getting ahead!*

Many parents believe that there's a benefit in *getting ahead* at KS3. I'm not sure I'd agree. GCSE is an educational bottleneck: everyone has to pass through it at the same time and at the same speed. Getting ahead at KS3 is like getting on an earlier train only to have to hang around at the next station waiting for a connection. The child who gets ahead often ends up treading water: this is a problem because it's very hard for a child to stay motivated in Y10 and Y11 if they feel they're not learning anything new. If your child finds KS3 easy, the educational decision looks like this: save the challenge for KS4 when your child really does need to stay motivated and engaged, or pull it into KS3 and risk your child switching off during a phase in the school journey that is far more important.

If your child finds school easy at KS3, this is not a bad thing. It means they have the time and space to do other things that they find stimulating and really enjoy. It creates more room for them to embed in their lives the sort of balance that will help them keep GCSEs in perspective.

I now teach in a mixed-ability comprehensive, but earlier in my career I worked at a very academic boys' school with an entrenched position at the top of the league tables. Pupils joined the school in Y9, and the question of stretch came up a lot during their first parents' evenings. *He seems to get his homework done very quickly,* some parents would say. *Great,* I'd reply, *he's got more time to relax or read something for fun.* The parents usually looked shocked and tried again: *I think he's finding it all a bit easy – could you give him something a bit more challenging?*

Sometimes I'd give the standard answer that the school curriculum would naturally become more demanding as the students progressed through the school. But sometimes – and especially if the parent pushed back – I'd be more blunt: *Forging ahead into GCSE content won't bring the return that you think. Once your child is into the throes of GCSE preparation, there'll be a daily pressure to do better, chasing the marginal returns of fine-grained detail. If you want him to have the energy and motivation to do this, it will do him good to remember a different experience in Y9. Looking back on the freedom he had then to do things he really enjoyed will help him remember that the exam slog is temporary. If he feels he's been grafting away on the same content for years, there's a much greater risk of growing stale and giving up.*

Sometimes the parents listened. Sometimes they didn't; sometimes they left the room with a sense of *huh!* in the air and signed their kid up for tutoring or some other sort of self-improving activity.

Was I right or was I wrong? For any individual child, it's a question that can only be answered on an individual basis, but I can tell you this: in this book you will hear the voices of teenagers who have suffered – and I mean *suffered* – during the exam experience. Ask yourself this question: if they'd had a chance to learn at KS3 the great benefit of stopping and saying *I've done enough – that's great; now I can do something else which I genuinely enjoy,* don't you think they would have had a much healthier, stronger force field around them when the GCSE years began?

Y12 Student: *Y7–9 – it's the time when you just want to have fun.*

- There is more freedom to have fun at KS3 than in KS4: if your child has spare time, how do they most like to spend it?
- What value do they get from this that they won't get from doing more schoolwork?

How do you react if it's not going OK?

Sometimes the mess of KS3 rears its head and your child will come home in tears. Over the years, most of the complaints that have come my way from KS3 parents have been variations on a theme: *something's gone wrong, there needs to be a clearer, tidier process so that this doesn't happen again*. Perhaps the issue was homework instructions and teachers setting them in different ways; sometimes it was communication and their child had got caught up in a clash between different sets of expectations and ended up in detention; most often it was friendships and all the jarring, messy difficulties of a much more complicated early-adolescence dynamic.

Schools do try to make the inevitably complex experience of KS3 a bit simpler and clearer for students: they do try to tidy things up and help students learn to understand the much more complicated environment they're now in, but it's worth being realistic that in KS3 there will be moments where the cogs don't turn smoothly. Often the bumps in the road are part of the learning: they are moments where you can help your child develop their maturity of thought by understanding that life doesn't fall into neat categories with simple sets of expectations which are equally easy for everyone to meet.

Most of the time at KS3, whatever has gone wrong is something reasonably minor. But it won't feel minor to your child: if, for example, they got let out late from a club or the lunch queue moved so slowly they didn't get anything to eat, your child might come home distraught, angry or both. For your child, the problem will feel like a real, significant problem: the way you react to this will inevitably set up patterns that shape how your child feels about other potential problems which might happen at school. So let's think now about how you can help your child learn to be calm, confident and constructive in dealing with the inevitable curveballs that will sometimes come their way.

★ Helping your child navigate problems

Whatever your thoughts on what your child is upset about, it's worth taking the time to listen for long enough before you react (see further, Chapter 4). If your child is upset, those feelings will need enough space to be heard and understood.

But after you've listened, you'll need to respond. Maybe your reaction goes one of two ways. Maybe you see how minor the incident is and you feel surprised at the scale of your child's reaction: *It's not the end of the world, there's no need to shout at your sister just because you had a bad day*. Or maybe you see the scale of your child's upset and you feel angry that the incident happened at all. *Of course there should have been time to have lunch! I'm going to email your Head of Year right now.*

You might be thinking *but this is supposed to be a book on exam stress – why are we talking now about clubs and lunch?* The two are related because exam stress is all about the uncertainty of *what happens if it doesn't go OK* (see further, Chapter 1). At KS3, when your child comes home from a day that didn't go well, your reaction is teaching them – implicitly – about what happens when something goes wrong. It's setting up a template that may come back into view whenever something goes awry: exam results and the lunch queue may seem unrelated, but the skills of knowing how to move through something upsetting or disappointing apply equally to both.

I've lost count of the number of students I've seen burst into tears over disappointing test results: like the slow-moving lunch queue, in the fullness of time an individual test score is rarely a disaster, but the emotions can be raw and difficult all the same. If your child is upset over something seemingly trivial, it's an opportunity to help them understand that feeling upset is a very real thing even if the problem isn't really a problem; we need to learn to be patient with our feelings and remember that they change over time. Give your child a hug, let them cry, tell them *some days are like this* and remind them that it will feel a bit better in the morning. If you do this, you'll help them learn that things going a bit wrong is disappointing, but it is survivable all the same.

If you're in the camp of *this shouldn't have happened at all, the school needs to do better*, you may have a point but you're setting a very high bar for your child about what counts as OK. When your child comes home with a disappointing mark in their History test, how do you want them to react? Do you want them to be interested in the mark, understand what went wrong and notice how to build on the good bits? Or do you want them to close down their thinking, flooded with guilt and shame and the feeling that this is *entirely unacceptable*? The bottom line is this: when mistakes happen in the school environment, do we take a balanced view of them, are we compassionate and realistic, or not?

> **Headteacher:** *Parents seem quicker to jump on a problem now – they go at it quicker and harder. When parents react, this impacts the kids: where is the threshold for what counts as a serious problem? If the lunch hall runs out of potatoes or the school bus is late, is this a serious problem? What is our tolerance for things not going well?*
>
> - Which sort of parent are you? Are you quick to jump on the email?
> - What does the alternative look like? What role-modelling would you be giving to your child if you waited for a bit, calmly comforted them, and helped them think about what they could do next to find a route through?

★ What to do if the problems aren't minor

But what happens if the problems at school aren't minor? What happens if my child is daily unhappy, and tells me they hate school? This is a very different scenario and needs careful – and early – attention.

★ Does your child have unrealistic expectations?

If your child is unhappy on a regular basis, it's worth trying to distinguish between two things: is it the situation or their expectations that are unmanageable? Children – and their parents – often have unrealistic expectations about how shiny, positive and successful the school experience should be. This often appears in social dynamics: if one child is mean to another, it's something that needs to be addressed, but your child may need your help in understanding that there's no easy route to bypass this altogether. Children often are mean: if your child is on the receiving end, it's often not their fault. If your child is upset because they've hurt someone else's feelings, this doesn't make them a bad person. Meanness is hurtful, yes, but it's an unfortunate yet fairly inevitable part of the process of learning about how to be kind. The same principle applies to schoolwork: if your child feels like they're not doing well enough, it may be because they have inappropriate expectations about the sorts of marks they should be getting.

If you think that a set of unrealistic expectations is causing your child's unhappiness, then patient, imaginative, empathetic discussion – using questions like the examples on p133 – will help them build a realistic, nuanced picture of what secondary school can be like. This will help them recalibrate their expectations into something more fulfillable and this is likely to make it much easier for them to be happy at school.

★ As a parent, do you need to rethink your own expectations?

KS3 may also be a time where – as a parent – you need to rethink your own expectations. Does your child feel they need to be something they are not? Are you asking them to achieve outcomes that may not be possible?

If your child is unhappy, this question is one of the most important to ask yourself (see further, Chapter 1).

When I think through each of the classes I've taught, there's usually been someone who has been told by their parents that they have to get certain grades. *My parents say that I have to get more than 80%. My parents say that anything less than an A isn't good enough.* I understand why parents say this, but it's usually based on thinking first about grades and then about the child. *Averaging over 80%*: sure, this looks like a great thing to aim for, but is the target fair and appropriate for your child? Or is it setting them up to feel like a failure even if they're trying really hard?

At KS3, your child will become increasingly self-aware: this means that they'll notice more clearly the gaps between who they are, how others appear to be and what seems to be important to the adults in their lives (see further, Chapter 1). It's these gaps that can cause a child to feel that they're not good enough. This is one of the reasons why thinking carefully about expectations will be central to the chapters about the public exam years. Fundamentally, there is no better way to motivate a child to work hard and make progress than to help them feel proud about what they have managed to achieve, rather than feeling distraught about not living up to expectations that may not have been appropriate in the first place.

★ Working constructively with the school

Unhappiness, however, isn't always the result of unrealistic expectations. Sometimes there's a fundamental misalignment between what the child needs and what's happening at school.

When a child's unhappiness stems from something that isn't working in the day-to-day environment at school and you can see that there's a genuine problem that needs action, rather than reframing, you'll need the school's help to address this. You'll need constructive dialogue with the school about what's going on. So, here's the final thing that you need at the ready: it's got to be possible for the school to be honest with you. *Of course they should be honest! It's their job!* Yes, but that doesn't always mean it's easy to do.

You'll get the best results from conversations with the school if it's possible for everyone to be open and realistic: the more understanding you are of the realities of secondary school life, the more constructive the conversations will be. If you go in aiming to blast your way to a result with anger and complaints, you'll make it harder for the school to be honest with you.

If you're unconvinced by this, then it's worth considering the following approaches: which one is likely to generate a better dialogue about what's actually happening? The parent who steams in, saying *it's outrageous this has happened, I can't believe you've let my child down in this way,* or the parent who opens with something like the following instead? *I understand that every school has pupils who are less happy than others; this doesn't always mean the school is doing a bad job. But I need you to be honest with me about how things are going; we all need to be realistic about whether or not we can help my child thrive in this environment or whether the fit just isn't right.* Wouldn't this sort of opening lead to much more constructive conversation about what your child needs?

> **Head of Y9:** *At KS3, parents often bury their heads in the sand because they don't want to believe it is a problem.*
>
> How would you know whether a problem is minor or more significant?
>
> Are school-related problems straightforward to assess on your own, or would it help to get guidance at an early stage from teachers and pastoral staff who understand the difference between *difficult-but-not-unusual* and *this-needs-specialist-help*?
>
> As a parent, what's your natural leaning: do you tend to downplay problems or do you assume the worst-case scenario instead?

But what about those KS3 exams...?

I've spent this chapter encouraging you not to think too much about exams at KS3 because it's much more important to focus on helping your child adjust to a more complex environment. It's for this reason that many schools encourage a light-touch approach to exams at this age. Revision is often built into lessons and there's much less emphasis on independent study than there will be at KS4.

No matter how light-touch the approach, however, exams are still exams. Your child will sit them and then they'll get to see their marks. As discussed in Chapter 3, formal school exams help to raise standards by making progress pinned-down, red-penned visible. But they also make the gaps more visible, they line all the students up and say *this one is 26% better than that one*. And so – at the end of a chapter which has encouraged you not to look much at the marks – we need now to move on to a chapter which spins back to that exam percentage. Because when the grade lands, you and your child will look at it, despite what you've read in this chapter.

Our next question, therefore, is this one: *when you and your child look at the KS3 exam results, how do you want your child to react?* Do you want them to see it only as a measure of success or failure, or would you rather help them see past the mark to the opportunities for learning and progress? Let's move on to Chapter 8.

> **Assistant Head, Teaching & Learning:** *We know that pupils will not read the comment if they see a grade. The grade is the first thing they look at. Then the second thing they look at is someone else's grade. The comment will be the last thing they look at.*
>
> - Does your child react in this way?
> - When you look at your child's school report, do you react in this way?

KEY IDEAS

- Secondary school is much more complicated than primary or junior school; you can help your child learn to adjust to the complex environment of KS3 if you talk to them about it at home. There are examples of useful questions you can ask your child on p133.
- Marks in exams should not be the main focus at KS3; the best way to work out how things are going is to think about the day-to-day process.
- KS3 is tiring and your child will need time to relax at home; if your child has a smartphone, it is worth thinking carefully about how much time they should spend on it.
- If your child finds school easy and you're looking for more stretch and challenge, there's not as much value in *getting ahead* as some parents think. There's probably more value in your child using the time for other things that they enjoy.
- There will be times when your child is upset by something that's happened at school; how you respond to this will create a template for how your child expects you to react if something goes wrong in general.
- Building a realistic understanding of what KS3 is like will help you support your child; it will also help you have open, honest conversations with the school about what your child needs.

CHAPTER 8

Tests and exams in Years 7–9; choosing GCSE subjects

Senior Deputy Head: *Pupils are always thinking about how others are doing, but trying to hide the hierarchy doesn't really work – they all know anyway.*

Exams are inherently stressful: that's an uncontroversial statement, but it's worth pausing just for a moment to ask *why?* Is it the exam that's so stressful or the judgement that comes with it? Is it the mark on the page that causes the heartbeat to quicken, or is it the fear of looking to the sides and finding out that other people did *better*?

This chapter will explore how KS3 students may be thinking about tests. I'll be explaining why it's unconstructive to focus too much on the hierarchy of who did better or worse, and I'll be outlining how you can help your child respond to their marks in a way that facilitates, rather than limits, future progress. At the end of the chapter, I'll be discussing how to support your child when they choose their GCSE options.

Why tests feel important, even at KS3

KS3 exams are often light-touch: you might hear your child's school refer to them as *low stakes* or something for the students to *take in their stride*.

Viewed objectively, any individual test at KS3 is a very small, arguably trivial, step along the way. But it often doesn't feel that way to the student. In this section, we'll be thinking about why.

> **Y9 Student:** *When I get really stressed, it feels like I'm lying down and there's something really heavy on my stomach. It feels like my breathing is more laboured.*
>
> How do exams make your child feel? Is this something they've talked about?

The pressure of the hierarchy

The defining feature of the exam experience is that it creates a hierarchy among students. That's its purpose: public exams take the nation's teenagers and line them up in rank order. KS3 exams are designed to be less significant: they are smaller and shorter, there's usually less for the student to do in terms of independent revision, and your child will probably sit them in a classroom rather than a large exam hall, but they create a hierarchy all the same. This means that no matter how friendly, supportive and positive the atmosphere, no matter how often someone says *it's just a test – there's nothing to worry about*, your child is still going to have to deal with all the feelings that the hierarchy brings with it.

Hierarchy is not a particularly attractive notion, but the concept is pulsing, instinctively, through an adolescent's veins. We're a herd species: our survival depends on being part of the pack. The inescapable reality is that teenagers are acutely alert to the herd hierarchy and who is valuable enough to be safe and secure within it. School grades – along with social media – are one of the most visible ranking metrics around. *Who came top? She did better than me. I beat him.* The language that teenagers use to talk about their results makes it quite clear that although their teacher might be reminding them *not to look to the sides* and to *run your own race*, the instinctive pull is to check out the line-up in the finishing positions.

It's not only the teenager who is interested in the ranking metrics. As a parent, if your child comes home after a test, the natural response is often *How did it go? What did you get?* It's very hard to resist the temptation to follow this up with *How did everyone else do?* I regularly hear anecdotes from schools about parents' WhatsApp groups which are hot with competitive interest: *Where's the top? Where's the bottom? What counts as OK?*

What this means for the child is that a test offers a triple dollop of judgement: the child's progress gets judged at school, this shapes how the child judges their own progress or worth and there's then a final round of judgement at home. There's no getting away from the fact that in the areas of life where grades matter, better grade outcomes do carry more value than lower grade outcomes. The problem is that young adolescents often still think in fairly blunt ways: it's easy for this message to get warped invisibly into the more problematic, generalised conclusion that *the people with those outcomes are more valuable overall than the people without them.*

> **Y9 Student:** *It's the pressure from other people and from teachers and how you'll get judged at home. Everyone's always being judged for what they do or how well they do. Everyone wants to be competing to see who's the best. After an assessment, everyone wants to know what you got.*
>
> Does your child tell you about how others reacted to their mark? How does this influence their own sense of how well they are doing?

Additional pressure: The connection with GCSE

KS3 tests can also feel surprisingly stressful to the student because they are a stepping stone to something much bigger. As Chapter 3 discussed, in order to raise outcomes it's become common practice in schools to start practising GCSE content and skills during KS3. Tests – especially in Y9 – might contain adapted GCSE questions, marking criteria is likely to echo the expectations of GCSE assessment, and teachers might provide a framing which helps students understand their marks in the context of what might happen as a GCSE outcome.

Making the connection clear between a KS3 school assessment and a Y11 GCSE exam is designed to improve exam technique but it can have an unfortunate consequence: it skews the perspective. It presents the two as directly connected even though there's lots in between. As teachers and parents, we know that there's miles of distance between a 12- and a 16-year-old: so much is going to happen and change during that time. But a 12-year-old student doesn't have the benefit of our retrospective perspective: they don't know what the next few years will be like; they don't know all the variables or how the process of working is going to become easier or harder as they get older. Referring too much to GCSEs can bring something into view that the child isn't old enough to be ready for; there's a risk that it makes everything heavier and more stressful.

The comments from the student below convey this idea; the student describes their experience at the start of Y10 but their comments are applicable to those moments in KS3 where GCSEs are already in view. This is why some of the advice in this chapter focuses on the idea of bringing the finish line closer and thinking about a positive next step that is localised to the here and now. If the end goal is *doing well at GCSE*, it can feel too far away to be motivating or too unknown for the child to feel reassuringly on track (see further, Chapter 5).

> **Student:** *What we were doing at the start of Y10 was connected directly to a set of exams in two years' time. At that point, you don't know what the exams are – you don't know what's going to be important, you don't know about what you will end up prioritising. It felt like it's all geared up to an end that you don't know.*
>
> What would your child say if you asked them whether they think their marks now are going to have an impact on their GCSE grades? How do they feel about this?

★ Talking about tests at KS3

From what you've read so far, you might be expecting me to suggest that at KS3, the solution is to pay no attention to tests at all, to suggest they don't matter in the slightest, never mention GCSEs and aim to avoid any comparison with other students' results. I'm not going to suggest this. It would be entirely unrealistic. Tests do exist, GCSEs are coming, comparisons with others are inevitable, some results are better than others. It would be pointless to try to pretend otherwise.

Instead, we need to help teenagers explore and find a route through these challenges, and this means we need to think about how we want to shape the way they talk about tests.

The light-touch nature of KS3 assessments means that you may not hear much about a test until after it's happened. If more formal sets of mid-year or end-of-year exams are announced, there'll probably be comparatively little expectation that students do significant amounts of independent revision. This is because independent revision takes maturity and it's a skill that is developed more as a child gets older. If your child's school does suggest that your child should be revising in advance, I'd encourage you to take a gentle interest in what they think they should do and why, but – at this age – it's probably counterproductive to make too big a deal of it. If your child is in a good rhythm for their everyday homework (see further, Chapter 5), their study habits will be about right for their age, whether or not you see them doing extra revision.

If you're looking for specific tips on how to help your child plan their revision, you might find the material in Chapters 9 and 10 useful, but please bear this in mind: if you make revision into too big a process when your child is in KS3, you'll turn it into something that feels difficult and heavy. This is likely to increase the stress levels as your child moves up into KS4 and – to repeat a familiar refrain – stress levels that are too high make it harder for your child to do well.

At KS3, therefore, most of the talking about tests will take place after they've happened and so it's worth thinking about which questions to ask when a child comes home. Different types of questions encourage your child to think about different types of things. The first list below contains questions or responses that bake in the more uncomfortable, counterproductive aspects of judgement, hierarchy and the long-term exam path; the second list are questions that will help your child understand and move through their feelings and think about how to make progress, enabling positive outcomes in the future.

★ Reponses that can be counterproductive

- *How did you do?* This focuses on the outcome; it suggests that the only thing that matters is the result. It loses sight of the fact that an interest in the process is what drives results forwards.
- *How did others do?* This increases the focus on the hierarchy; it suggests to the child that you, the parent, care about whether or not they are better than others.
- *You'd better work harder next time.* This advice lacks boundaries; it doesn't offer a clearly defined target that the child can meet. It leaves undefined how much work is needed to meet expectations.
- *That's a really disappointing mark.* If the mark's disappointing, your child is probably already feeling disappointed. A comment like this cements the feeling and can easily sound like criticism. If a child feels in trouble for their mark, the pressure to do well increases and they are less likely to be honest with you if they think they need help.
- *Don't you know that this is leading towards your GCSE course? If you don't take it seriously now, what's going to happen to your GCSE grade?* This question shifts the focus to something that is too far away for your child to understand and ends with an unanswerable blank about what the problematic outcome might be. It's more likely to demotivate than motivate because it doesn't focus on a next step that is close enough to be achievable.

Y9 Student: *There's a lot at stake because some people think that if they are about to fail, then their futures are about to be messed up.*

- What's your reaction to this? Do you think the Y9 student is right to think that results at KS3 can mess up someone's future?
- Would your child agree with this Y9 student or not?

★ Responses that are more constructive

As is the case for all the suggested conversation structures, these questions are not designed to be asked all at once. It's a selection of the types of questions you could ask: you'll soon find out through trial and error which types are likely to be most constructive for your child.

- *What was the test on?* This question encourages engagement with the material; it helps the child make progress because it creates another opportunity for the child to think about the subject content, using their own words to describe what they've been doing and what they got asked.
- *Tell me about your mark: what do you think it means? Did your teacher give any advice about how to interpret it? Remember, the mark itself means very little; understanding it in its context is the important thing.* This response reminds the child that context matters; it encourages them to remember that 70% on an easier test is not always better than 60% on a harder test. Taking time to interpret a percentage helps your child learn to think about what a mark means for them.
- *How do you feel about your mark?* This response creates the space for your child to voice their own disappointment or pride. This helps you join them in celebrating what has gone well and it also increases the likelihood that – if things haven't gone well – they will look to you for support rather than pull away because they fear blame.

- *How do you feel about how others did?* This question creates the opportunity for your child to talk through their feelings about the inevitable intra-class competition. It creates room to be sympathetic if your child is starting to feel demoralised, reducing the risk that demoralisation builds into disengagement.
- *What were the things that went well in this test? What does this show you about study-habits that are worth repeating? Is there anything you think you should do differently for the next test?* This prompts balanced reflection; it reminds the child that a disappointing mark doesn't mean that everything went wrong. It helps the child think about what they can build on and how they can make changes. It offers a sense of empowerment; this is much more likely to motivate the child. It focuses on specific, achievable changes rather than an open-ended suggestion to just *work harder*.
- *If your teachers are talking about GCSEs, I know this can make it seem more important, but there's still a long time left until then. GCSEs are tomorrow's story, not today's. The thing to focus on is what to do next: let's keep this manageable – what do you think would be a good thing to do now?* This helps to bring the view down to a manageable size; it's more likely to motivate your child to think meaningfully about a positive next step that is straightforwardly attainable.

★ What does the best next step look like?

Sometimes parents ask me how they'll know what the best next step is for their child after a disappointing test result. It's a fair question, but the response is that as a parent you don't need to have the answers for the route map for academic progress. That's the teacher's job. As a parent, your role is to help your child learn to think independently about the process, and to help them maintain the physical and emotional energy needed to keep doing the work. Let's explore this further.

Maintain physical and emotional energy: this is important. Sometimes the best next step has nothing to do with schoolwork at all: sometimes a child needs the counterbalance of doing something else that is positive, energising and overall motivation-boosting. Sometimes a child needs to hear their parent say *I'm so sorry to hear you've had a rough day at school and I understand why you're disappointed about this test. But I want you to remember that a geography test is only one little bit of your life: when I look at you, I see so much more than your marks in a test. I see your sense of fun, your creativity, and all the other things that I love about you. Your geography test mark is a snapshot of how much you know about that bit of geography today – it doesn't define anything more than that. When the dust has settled on this test, we can think about what to do next to move things forwards.*

Learn to think independently about the process: this is equally important, but perhaps it sounds a little vague. Here's what I mean: if your child is disappointed by their mark, when they're ready to think about how to do better the next time, you could use a question like one of these to help them think about what to do next:

- *Did your teacher give you any advice about what to do next? Why do you think they suggested this?*
- *If you could wave a magic wand and know one bit of this material perfectly, which bit would you choose and why?*
- *Let's think about the next lesson for this subject: what would help this go well? Would you like to tell me about what you did in the last lesson so that it's fresh in your mind for the next one?*
- *Progress is all about taking one step at a time: let's think about something small you could do to move things forwards just a little bit. How about setting a ten-minute timer: what useful thing could you do in that time?*

The benefit to asking your child questions like these is that if you are interested in what your child thinks, they'll learn to think more carefully about how they learn. You'll be helping them upskill in self-review, planning and decision-making and this will help them get better and better at working independently.

If your child finds these questions difficult to answer, you'll get to see which bits of the process they feel less comfortable with. This will give you an insight which helps you communicate effectively with the teacher about the support your child needs.

> **11–18 SENDCO:** *Breaking the next step down to something that's a manageable size really helps. It means they can get started – they can get on with this bit.*
>
> What is going to help your child feel clearer and more motivated about how to move forwards: giving a vague instruction to *do better*, or taking an interest in something specific that they can do right away?

★ Targeted strategies for different %

The reaction that your child has to a KS3 exam mark will start to embed habits that they'll take with them into KS4. Unfortunately, no KS3 child has an innate understanding of how their educational experience will change over time and the skills that will set them in good stead for the future. The principles below will help you unpick some of the potentially problematic reactions that your child might have; they'll enable you to help your child respond in a way that is constructive in the long term.

The principles are calibrated to different percentages. **I cannot say often enough that at KS3 the percentages themselves tell you comparatively little.** I've data-tracked thousands of internal exam results in my career: 70% in one assessment can be very different from 70% in another. But regardless of this, the percentages always shape how the child views their own progress and this is why conversations can make a big difference to the attitude that your child carries forwards with them.

> **Assistant Head, Teaching & Learning:** *Sometimes there's an 'OMG I've failed' approach when they get an assessment back. We get hugely emotional responses to internal exams – a lower grade suddenly seems like the worst thing in the world – they can't quite cope with the difference between where they are now and where they are aiming to get to.*
>
> - How does your child respond to their KS3 marks? Can they see beyond them and think about what comes next, or do they get overwhelmed by the feelings that the marks produce?

★ 59% or below

I need to repeat my message that an individual percentage at KS3 tells you comparatively little about likely outcomes 3–5 years down the line. If your child comes home with a low-ish mark in KS3, don't make the mistake of pressing a mental panic button in your head, firing off queries about tutors or telling your child that they're never gaming or going out with their friends again. Sometimes a low mark comes from an assessment that was inappropriately difficult, sometimes it's the result of developmental differences that will even out over time, sometimes it's as simple as the fact that your child missed the class revision lesson.

But I am going to tell you that when I was tracking pupil progress as a senior leader, I was always concerned when students had multiple marks which were noticeably low, and especially so if they were south of 45%. A low mark does not always mean that your child can't or won't be able to do French, History or whatever it is, but it does mean they've had the experience of not-knowing more than they do know. And this is a problem for two reasons: first, at this age it's demoralising and the natural tendency then is to pull away, trying less hard rather than harder. Second, the quantity of not-known material makes it much harder to work out what to prioritise and focus on next. Score 95% and it's very obvious what to focus on next. But score 43/100 and the decision is harder. Why choose this bit, not that bit? It's for these reasons that a sub-50% mark could cause a reduction in progress.

What to do, then, as a parent? I repeat my advice: hold back on the panic button for a moment. Wait and see if the mark is isolated; take a sympathetic interest in how your child is feeling. *On a scale of 1–10, how are you feeling about this?* If they are gutted, give them a hug, remind them that some days are like this. But – when the sting of the disappointment has softened a bit – it's worth taking an interest in how clear they feel about what to do next.

> **Student:** *I felt too stressed out and overwhelmed to even open the textbook. It was like having a completely messy room and you don't know where to start to tidy it up. I had so much to do, I couldn't even begin to decide where to start.*
>
> Does your child feel this way sometimes?

★ Supporting the next steps

If your child is at ease and confident about the route forwards, then it's probably a situation that will solve itself. But if they are vague – *I've just got to work harder* – try to help them move through this to a clearer, more specific, more attainable goal. *Let's put some specifics on this: you can't finish a to-do list unless you know what it looks like. Give me an example of one thing you'd like to focus on and why.* If the answer stays vague or tips into the anger that reveals it's all getting too much – *I dunno – it's just everything – I don't want to talk about it – get off my case!* – then you need help from the school.

You need the school's advice, but you need to make sure that you get something focused and manageable for your child, not advice on the totality of what has to be done. *Here's the syllabus outline; they should know pp53–72 in this textbook.* This won't help your child. You need their advice on what to do next. *I need specific, boundaried next steps. I reckon my child can do 30 minutes each weekend on this. What's your guidance for a focus that's manageable and achievable within that framework?* What you need from the school is a way to help your child look past a whole pile of unknowns, get started on something, and be motivated by the progress that they'll then start to make.

★ Balancing out the disappointment

The final thing to bear in mind is the principle of balance. Getting most of the answers wrong is like getting repeatedly punched. *Wrong! Wrong again! Still wrong!* Worse than that, it's socially demoralising because – unless the assessment really was a massive misfire – most of the class won't be sub-50%, for all of the educational reasons I've set out on p158.

If sub-50% is a situation that repeats and it gradually becomes clear that high exam marks really aren't your child's thing, then think about the balance of how you'd like their life to feel. *They're going to have to work harder, we'd better get tutors – look, you can't go out at the weekend while your marks are like this.* Maybe. But if you go down this route, what you are doing is upping the proportion of your child's life that feels miserable and removing the balance of the bits they enjoy.

So how about this instead? *Does it feel like school sucks? OK, I get it. It's worth slogging on so that you pass, but let's set limits around it. Let's decide the hours of the day when you'll be working. Let's decide a reasonable set of expectations about what it's possible to do in that time. When you've met those, you're done, regardless of whether or not there's more you could do. And then let's write a list of all the things that will be far more enjoyable that you can do when you're not in the work zone. Let's make sure there's enough of the fun stuff so that schoolwork doesn't feel like it's all there is. You've got to take your GCSEs, yes, but there is much more to life than just that. We'll set limits around work so that it doesn't overwhelm.*

Put yourself in your child's position. In which scenario do you think you'd be more motivated to keep going? In which scenario do you think you'd be happier?

★ 60–85%

Maintaining a balanced perspective

Remember all that stuff from Chapter 6 about the brain's tendency to think in simple generalisations as the default mode? Simple generalisations are the only mode for a young child and the work of adolescence is partly to develop our ability to move from a blunt, one-dimensional response into something more accurate and nuanced. *He's a baddie.* Not quite, he's actually someone who does a range of actions, some good, some less good, and different people will view him in different ways. *I got stuff wrong.* Maybe, but your answer was a blend of right and wrong and we need to think about both.

In the 60–85% bracket, your child's answers will have been a mixture of good and bad, but the KS3 young, generalising brain is likely to focus on one category only, and because the focus at school during exam hand-back is typically how to improve, they'll probably focus on what they got wrong. This can be the beginnings of the type of catastrophisation that the student describes on p164 and it's highly problematic because it makes students do worse, not better.

★ Building on strengths; avoiding underachievement

Let me explain: what does *underachievement* mean? *Less than they could have done.* Correct, and what this means is that a student didn't use what they knew to best effect. Imagine a student whose attention habitually zooms in on what they don't know rather than what they do; this is the student who is so distracted by what they're about to get wrong that they aren't able to get maximum benefit by thinking about and squeezing the juice from what they can remember and do understand.

If your child comes home with a 60–85% score, be aware of the risk posed by the wish to improve. Reduce the mistakes, notice the knowledge gaps, yes – this is part of it – but this has to be balanced with being clear and confident about what is already secure. Lessons will focus on the mistakes and the gaps, so at home, your role is to help your child develop their capacity to maintain a balanced view. *I got 71% – the problem was that waves came up and I couldn't remember that section. – Oh I see,* you could say, *it sounds like you now know what to prioritise in your revision next time – that's a good thing. But tell me about the stuff that went right: which questions were the easiest ones? Which material do you think you know best so far?* Wouldn't that help your child keep a balanced perspective that doesn't lose sight of what they're already getting right?

> **Head of History:** *I think this idea that they do not know enough comes from each other – they get very stressed when they think that others know more than they do.*
>
> - What does your child tell you about first? The things they got right or the things they got wrong? What does this show you about what they're focusing on more?

★ 85% or above

This one's easy, you might think. *It's going great! They just need to keep it up!* Please, if your child is smashing scores in or near the 90s, think twice about telling them to *keep it up*. Remember, children want to do well – they'll naturally want to maintain their position at the top of the class. What they don't know is that being at the top of the class is going to look and feel different as they get older. Scores in the 90s are possible at KS3 and – for a much smaller number of students – they are possible at KS4. But they are far less likely to be possible in the sixth form, highly improbable at university and in real life as a whole, I don't know anyone who thinks *today, in adult-ing, I nailed 97%.*

When teenagers progress through school and their marks go down because syllabus content is harder, they often find this demoralising. It's really, really difficult to be proud of your progress if the marks appear lower. This means that the most helpful message you can give your high-scoring KS3-er is to help them build a balanced perspective on the downsides of high scores and the upsides of this changing. *Well done*, you could say, *that's cracking – sounds like you found the questions straightforward. This is proof of your concentration in class and hard work and we're so proud of the way your approach is working out for you. But I wonder whether finding it easy makes it boring at times? Do you think that if the questions were harder, and your scores were lower, that would increase the interest and the opportunity for growth? It might feel less comfortable but there'd be an upside. I'm mentioning this because if you're keen to stay ambitious, you'll end up doing difficult things and this means your scores will be lower. It's worth being aware of this in advance.*

> **Assistant Head, Teaching & Learning:** *We've been talking to the students about their attitude to mistakes. One of the answers that stuck with me was the idea of, 'Why would you want to make a mistake?'*
>
> If you asked your child how many mistakes it's OK to make, what would they say?
> Do you think your child has a balanced, realistic understanding of how inevitable and necessary mistakes are?

★ Being realistic about mistakes

It's also worth being interested in your child's perception of their mistakes. A constructive relationship with mistakes is essential for progress (see further, Chapter 5). At KS3 it's worth understanding that a child who is on 85% or above already understands things well enough to feel that it'd be very attainable to do even better. You might hear them saying that they *can't believe they got that question wrong* or that they could *easily get it right the next time.* Feedback in class always looks at how to move forwards: *here's how to get more right* is always the message. But I can tell you that in years and years of trailing through KS3 exam percentages, it is incredibly rare for anyone ever to get 100%. The higher the score, the harder it is to push it upwards: no matter how well your child knows the content and how hard they work, there will almost certainly still be some mistakes. That's just the way it goes.

> **Y9 Student:** *If you're someone who likes to do well, it's really hard to get a bad result because doing well is something you pride yourself on. Getting a bad result makes you feel like a core part of your identity is being challenged.*
>
> If your child usually gets high scores, what do they think counts as a *bad result* for them? What does this show you about your child's ability to tolerate getting something wrong?

★ Avoiding perfectionism

If you want to avoid inculcating the sort of counterproductive perfectionism that can develop into problematic hyper-engagement, encourage your child to be realistic and help them learn to be compassionate about the careless mistake that they feel they shouldn't have made. It probably wasn't careless, and yes, if they'd been looking at that question in isolation and not in the heat of the exam, they probably could have got it right. But that doesn't mean they *should* have worked harder and they *should* be cross with themselves for getting things wrong. They may well be irked at the brain's glitches, that's a natural response, but encourage them not to see it as a personal failing when it happens. High-attaining students are often unskilled in mistake-making because they don't make very many of them. These students need to practise accepting that mistakes do – and always will – happen, especially if you're ambitious and keen to do something challenging and difficult.

> **Y13 Student:** *I definitely catastrophise, I definitely feel that if I make a mistake then I've failed the whole thing. 100% you catastrophise about how it's gone. I know loads of people feel this way.*
>
> - If your child gets high scores, could you use the evaluative thinking technique on p120 to help them learn to keep their mistakes in perspective?
> - Would this help them avoid the risk of developing a catastrophising mindset as they get older?

Choosing GCSEs

The final act of KS3 is to choose GCSEs. I say *final* – it isn't really because it probably happens in January to March, but it's the decision that symbolises one thing is ending and something else is beginning. It's also a moment that creates framing for the GCSE experience: it's the moment when the GCSE conversation becomes personalised. Rather than *GCSEs* in general, your child will be thinking about *their* GCSEs. Their actual GCSEs. The GCSEs that are going to be there on their CV *forever*. In this final section on KS3, therefore, let's think about which types of framing are constructive.

How much does the subject combination matter?

Opening question: does it really matter which subjects your child picks? *Yes!* Are you sure about this? Are you sure that the choice of subjects will have any direct link to a part of your child's life that absolutely has to be there for them to thrive as an adult? Or is there a much wider margin of tolerance than the apparent importance of the decision might imply?

Students sometimes find it difficult to pick their options: pros and cons each way, maybe no clear front-runners. *Toss a coin, then*, I'd tell them if they asked my opinion. When they realised I was being serious, they sometimes questioned the advice. *I know it sounds flippant – if you'll forgive the pun*, I'd say, *but if there are no clear best options then they're all equally sound. You might as well save yourself the stress of the decision.*

I'm not sure anyone ever did take my coin-flipping advice, but let's take a clear look at the counterfactuals. Let's think about the child who is uneasy about their decision, caught in the confusion of *my mum says, my dad says, my mum's friend who's a doctor says, my neighbour's daughter's now at university and she says*. Let's think about their framing: the choice of GCSEs appears difficult to get right because of the risk of multiple possible consequences which may or may not apply. Then let's think about the same child flipping that coin, confident in the belief that there's a wide margin of tolerance: lots of routes exist throughout life and each one has their benefits. The choice is yours: which scenario sends a better message about the scale of risk that you'd like your child to associate with the idea of GCSEs?

★ Think about the process, not the outcome

I'm only half serious about flipping a coin: it's good for your child to have the experience of making a decision which may feel like one of the most significant decisions of their life so far. But I would encourage you to keep an eye on the framing, and when you're helping your child think it through, I'd encourage you to steer clear of the *ifs* and the *buts* of what might happen 10 years down the line.

Instead, I'd encourage you to come back to the here and the now, focusing on the process: which homework does your child typically do first? Which subjects do they talk about most at home? Who knows exactly how things will pan out multiple years later, but here's a certainty you can hold on to: if your child is more engaged with this subject than that one, it'll offer them more return in terms of their academic and personal growth, whatever your colleague's nephew who's *already got an offer from a law firm* thinks.

> **Headteacher:** *I'd love all schools to prioritise the controllables – i.e. attitude and approach to study – rather than the uncontrollables – i.e. outcomes.*
>
> Do you agree with this headteacher? If you agree, what are your reasons? If not, why not?

KEY IDEAS

- Children often feel anxious about tests because they feel they'll be judged by teachers, their peers and their parents.
- Adolescents are instinctively concerned about how they fit into the class hierarchy.
- If students believe there is a direct connection between KS3 tests and GCSEs, this can make the tests feel more significant than they are.
- The way you talk about KS3 tests at home will impact your child's relationship with exams. Asking questions – such as those on p154 – will help your child learn to respond to tests in a constructive way.
- If test results are disappointing, you can help your child by focusing on a manageable, specific next step.
- You can support your child by helping them to keep a balanced perspective about the things that are going well and the things that are going less well.
- It is better to choose GCSEs based on what is going well in the present rather than focusing too much on what might happen in the future.

CHAPTER 9

Creating positive expectations and a constructive work rhythm in Year 10

Student: *My stress probably started in Y10 – it started to get real.*

At KS4, all the ingredients in the exam-stress mix start to move up a gear: the daily mention of GCSE exams increases, potentially bringing with it the heavy feeling that there'll be a direct and long-lasting impact on future success. Then there's the mood swings, frustrations and vulnerability of adolescence, making it harder to talk about or tolerate the risk that exams might deliver a painfully disappointing result.

Chapter 10 will discuss the nuts and bolts of getting work done, whether a tutor is needed, and the strategies that will facilitate effective revision habits. This chapter focuses on the looming view of GCSEs: I'll be outlining how to help your child maintain a healthy perspective and build a constructive work rhythm in advance. On p182, you'll find guidance about what to do if you have serious concerns about your child's well-being.

> **11–18 SENDCO:** *The students are putting pressure on themselves and they're hearing about the exams all the time from everyone else. 'In the exam' – they are probably hearing this 3–4 times a lesson and they've got 5 lessons a day. That's 20 times hearing those words a day – easily.*
>
> By the end of Y10, your child will be hearing about exams multiple times each day. How would you feel if someone reminded you of a deadline 20 times in one day?

Thinking about expectations

As a parent, when your child starts KS4, it's useful to take a long, questioning look at your own beliefs about how you'd like your child to do. These beliefs are going to impact your child's relationship with their results, whether you intend this or not (see further, Chapter 1).

As your child moves into KS4, the risk becomes more acute of a problematic mismatch between your expectations and the reality of your child's current – or likely – grades. This is because grade projections get more accurate as your child gets older. Whether or not your child received target GCSE grades at KS3, at some point in Y10 there'll be a much clearer, sharper indication of the grades your child might get.

Your expectations as a parent might already be clearly stated: *We're an A-grade family; I've told him he should match what his sister got last year.* But they might be hiding, lurking in the shadows of what your own experience throws up as the benchmark. Your expectations will shape your reaction when you – as the parent – see these grades. This is true whether or not you have consciously verbalised to yourself what your expectations are. If you've already felt that sudden jolt of surprise, surfacing uninvited and leaving you with the unsettling feeling of *oh – that wasn't quite what I was expecting*, you'll know what I mean.

> **Child and Adolescent Psychotherapist:** *Some parents say that they don't mind what their children get, but a lot of what is going on here is below the surface, it's unconscious. Parents do care about academic results, even if they say they don't, and children still pick up on the fact that parents want them to do well. Caring about academic success exists whether you're saying it out loud or not.*
>
> • As a parent, do you think this psychotherapist is right? Are you ever surprised by caring more about something school-related than you thought you would?

What if predictions don't match expectations?

If there's a mismatch between your expectations and your child's likely outcomes, your child will probably notice this. Maybe you try to hide it by saying brightly, *Well, perhaps these predictions are normal at this stage – 25% of the school's GCSE outcomes are grade 7 or above – it's probably going to improve next year – I've heard that school really ramps up in Y11.* But your child will probably still pick up on your sense of surprise all the same, with its accompanying, but perhaps unintentional, flavour of *you're not delivering what I hoped you would.* Once disappointment is in the mix, there's a risk that your child starts to feel like a failure; this can lead to disengagement, making it much harder for them to do well (see further, Chapter 5).

★ Working out what your expectations are

The questions below will help you think about what your expectations are and where they come from. It's helpful to do this in the early stages of Y10 so that you've thought through your expectations *before* your child gets their first set of predicted grades.

1. **What GCSE grades do you think your child will get?** Why do you think this? Is it based on indications from school reports,

or is it influenced by your own grades, someone else's grades such as a sibling or cousin, or average outcomes for your child's school?
2. **What GCSE grades would you like them to get?** What are the reasons for this?
3. **What GCSE grades do you think they *need* to get?** What are you using as the benchmark for *need*? Is it tied to a particular career or university destination? What makes this *necessary* rather than *preferable*?
4. **What's the baseline for it being *just about OK?*** Let's put the idea of a preferred outcome on one side for the moment: where's the tipping point from *suboptimal* into *problematic*? Is it the grades required for entry to sixth form? Does it have to be this? Could it be lower? How low could it go and there *still* be a route through?

> **Y12 Student:** *Where did the pressure at GCSE come from? If you've got a parent who did well themselves, they can put that pressure on you – they expect you to get the same grades.*
>
> Do you expect your child to get the same grades as you? Do you expect them to do better?
> If your child does less well than you did, how would you respond? Why do you think you'd respond in this way?

★ Widening the margin of tolerance

Whenever I run an event for parents on exam stress, it's not unusual for the atmosphere to become slightly uncomfortable when we get to the idea of a baseline for it being *just about OK*. I can almost see the thought bubbles voicing a prickly resistance: *Are you suggesting that we drop our standards?*

No, I'm not: pausing to think about what is survivable is not an invitation to slacken off and say *if I can still manage with those grades, there's no point aiming for anything higher*. Children usually want to do well: if they think they can make it, they'll probably try. Disengagement and *not bothering* happens when a target feels out of reach or when the cost of trying becomes too great (see further, Chapter 5). Thinking about what is survivable is an exercise in noticing the margin of tolerance and remembering that there's usually significant distance between *not exactly as I'd hoped* and *this is a disaster*.

The idea of widening the margin of tolerance is a key idea in this book. In the long run-up to GCSEs, your child has to carry the risk that the GCSE grades might *not* be as hoped. This risk is real: as I said in Chapter 6, I have never, ever made a set of predictions that were an exact match for the outcomes. The more fixed and narrow the set of expectations, the smaller the target. The smaller the target, the greater the risk. The greater the risk, the greater the stress. The greater the stress, the harder it is to work effectively and do well.

So, as a parent, I'd encourage you to think carefully about this: do you really want to talk only about the ideal outcome, embedding the idea that getting the grades needed for a particular sixth form is the *only* thing that matters? Or do you want to talk in a way that keeps reminding your child that *yes, it'd be great to make the sixth form or whatever the ideal result looks like, but let's remember that other routes through life are possible all the same. If you don't get the grades, the disappointment will be understandable, but temporary because there are multiple ways to live a fulfilling life. You'll be developing your skills and getting benefit from the process of working for GCSEs even if the grades don't match what you're hoping for. Let's not lose sight of this.* Wouldn't this help your child feel safer? Wouldn't it make it easier for them to maintain a healthy balance? Don't you think it'd be *more* straightforward for your child to keep trying hard if they believe that there's *less* of a risk of a painful, lingering sense of failure at the end of it all?

> **11–18 Inclusion Lead:** *I'd want all kids to know that they are going to make mistakes and that's OK; they'll learn from these. I'd say to them, please have a Plan B. If adults talked a bit more about Plan B, about when they ended up with Plan B because Plan A didn't work out and it was all OK, that would help. When adults share their stories, it really helps pupils feel that Plan B can be OK.*
>
> - Do you share your stories with your child about a Plan B that turned out to be OK in the end?
> - What does Plan B look like for your child? Have you helped them notice its upsides? (See further, Chapter 6.)

Establishing a balanced perspective

The dominant ingredient of KS4 is that your child will start to hear about GCSEs all the time. Ask your child how often they hear the words *in the exam* or *GCSE* or *mark scheme*. Whatever the frequency is at the start of Y10, it's only going to increase as they move through to Y11.

It's entirely likely that the school will also be reminding pupils of the importance of maintaining a healthy balance between work, rest, exercise, socialising, etc., but that doesn't mean that the KS4 experience in school isn't inherently imbalanced. Your child will probably spend more than 70% of their time at school in the classroom, and the prospect of GCSEs is going to take up more focus than anything else.

Parents often feel that in order to support their child with school, they need to double up what's happening at school by repeating the processes or messages at home. You might be invited to help your child with revision, testing them on key content or making sure they have access to recommended revision resources, ensuring that what you do at home reinforces what is happening at school. This is an important part of how you can support them at home. But – as GCSEs dominate increasingly at school – there's also a need for your contribution at home to act as the counterbalance for the necessarily exam-focused experience at school. This is especially necessary if your child is prone to single-mindedness or they have a tendency to hyper-focus on just one thing at a time.

> **Senior Leader (Pastoral):** *We need to frame assessments more calmly: grades are important but not hugely important; we need to help students understand this.*
>
> - If you asked your child how important GCSEs are on a scale of 1–10, what would their answer be?
> - Do you think you would agree with their evaluation? What does this show you about the difference between your child's perspective and yours?

★ Focusing on things beyond GCSEs

Each individual GCSE syllabus will have been carefully designed to develop knowledge and skills that are important for that subject; the broad range of subjects create the opportunity for students to develop educationally in many different ways. Whenever I look at a syllabus design, I'm usually really impressed by what it sets out to achieve.

The problem is, however, that it doesn't always feel that way to the teenager who's sitting in the classroom, practising a particular bit of the syllabus *again*. To many children, GCSEs feel like they're largely a test of who could keep listening in class even when they were bored, who managed to learn large blocks of seemingly arbitrary content accurately, and who was good at remembering instructions and delivering exactly what they'd been told to say.

If your child finds regular, meaningful value in their GCSE subjects, that's great. But if they don't, they'll feel much better overall if they don't lose sight of the meaningful value in the other parts of their life.

The questions below create the opportunity to balance out the perspective by thinking about things that matter *beyond* GCSEs. I'm not suggesting that you sit your child down for an interview-esque grilling; the questions are there to indicate the types of things that it'll be useful to encourage your child to think about from time to time. This will help them remember that GCSEs matter, but they're not the only thing that's important in life.

1. **What do you value** most in the people who matter to you?
2. **Which characteristics** matter most in the workplace?
3. **Which dispositions or attitudes** help someone through difficult times in their own life?
4. **Which skills** help someone form close and supportive relationships with others?

The answers are, of course, fairly subjective and there's probably some overlap between what GCSE develops and what life in its broader sense requires: reliability, skills in listening, accuracy over detail – these are attributes which are useful in the exam room and elsewhere. But there'll probably be plenty in the answers which is noticeably absent from the GCSE experience. A sense of humour, for example, compassion, empathy in day-to-day interactions, a cheerful readiness to see the benefits of what's available in the present rather than always pushing for something just that little bit *better* – these aren't really part of the game plan for getting extra marks in the exam.

Helping your child maintain a balanced perspective by thinking about things that matter *beyond* GCSEs will benefit your child, whatever their relationship with work. It will help them keep a broader perspective, noticing and valuing other aspects of their own identity; it will also help them see the value of establishing healthy boundaries around when to start – and when to stop – working.

★ Disengagement: Creating a counterbalance

A counterbalance is especially important if your child feels like school isn't for them: feeling like a failure can be the beginning of all sorts of potentially problematic behavioural patterns such as disengagement, rebellion, or distracting thrill-seeking elsewhere. If school is a difficult experience for your child, there's powerful value in making sure there are other parts of their life that offer them something different, where they feel they can comfortably meet the expectations of the people around them.

A few years ago, my job involved raising standards of behaviour in the classroom. I had a steady flow of students through my office who were in trouble because they hadn't behaved appropriately in class. I'd go through the usual procedures, set action plans and follow-ups, but I'd also try to make sure they understood that school rules were specific to school, not the blueprint for life. I'd tell them that cracking jokes with their mate while the teacher was talking was a problem in the context of a Maths lesson but that they shouldn't lose sight of the value in other contexts of having a sense of humour or being tightly connected to their friends. *Don't forget,* I'd say, *that if I'd been born in ancient Sparta, I'd have been bottom of the pile: I can't throw straight or run that fast. Being good at Maths would have been an irrelevance. Different skills matter in different contexts – you're at school right now and I'd recommend that you don't end up back in my office again because of your behaviour in class – but you won't be at school forever. Know what you're good at and find the right context for this.*

> **Housemaster:** *In terms of my main pastoral concerns, exam stress is probably third on the list after sex and drugs, but it's linked to both of these because self-esteem in the classroom feeds into this. Kids who feel that they are not doing as well as they should are more likely to be drawn into ways to feel better. Every case I've encountered as a Housemaster of misuse of drugs, alcohol, risky sex – all of these have come from students who feel they are not doing well enough.*
>
> - What is your child best at? Does this get valued as much and as clearly as it should?

★ Counterbalancing, not undercutting

I need to be clear, though: keeping GCSEs in perspective means providing a counterbalance that brings other things into view. It doesn't mean undercutting the messaging at school. Five days a week, your child will hear that GCSEs matter – and they do. If your child seems to be overwhelmed by it all, it's probably not helpful to try to mitigate this by a 180 pivot which pulls in the opposite direction.

They don't really matter at all! This is just as untrue as the equally unbalanced message that *they're the be-all and end-all*. The balanced message is to say *Yes, they're in view right now – they're probably the most significant thing you've done so far at school, but this is tied to today's context. Other things matter too and the importance of GCSEs gets smaller and smaller as you move beyond them. This situation is temporary, so let's work out the best way through it and remember that it passes.*

> **Student:** *I think some of the other messaging doesn't help: the messaging that your GCSEs don't matter – this feels like it invalidates the feelings. It's not helpful to hear they don't matter.*
>
> Think about something that you've been told is important: how would you feel if someone else said it didn't matter at all?

Establishing an effective work rhythm

KS4 is educationally different from KS3. This isn't just because GCSEs are closer, it's also because children are older. This means that there are different expectations for homework. Most schools aim for homework to be comfortably manageable at KS3. This is partly because children are younger and haven't yet developed their own time management skills, and it's partly because – as discussed in Chapter 7 – there is so much else to get used to in KS3 that it's best if there's plenty of time to decompress at home at the end of the school day.

At KS4, things are a bit different. Homework timetables are often designed to help students develop their skills in time management; homework might be set with longer deadlines so that there's more room to practise choosing when to do it; the more advanced nature of curriculum content means that homework tasks might be longer and students might need to subdivide a piece of work over different days. There's also the added complexity of optional extras. Perhaps your child's school suggests micro-revision on a daily basis throughout KS4 or perhaps their lesson resources include links to additional materials for students who'd like to go a bit further or do a bit extra.

Put simply, in KS4 there is more choice about what to do and when to do it. Increasing the choice is a necessary part of helping teenagers become more independent in the way they learn. The challenge is that some teenagers are naturally good at this and some aren't. This means that, as a parent, you may need to help your child learn how to plan their time effectively; the next section will help you with this.

★ The importance of planning when to work

I'm going to focus on the idea of planning *when to work*. I'm going to suggest that this question should come first and that the granular details of what tasks are on the to-do list should come second.

This may feel counter-intuitive: most people write a to-do list first, and then allocate time to the tasks. Unfortunately, writing the to-do list first can create several problems:

- **overload:** if a student thinks about *what* they need to do and then *when* to do it, there's a real risk that the to-do list starts to overwhelm. The risk of overwhelm is because – at school – the to-do list is shaped by someone else's expectations and it may or may not be a suitable shape for your child's capacity.
- **procrastination:** starting off the planning process by writing a to-do list can also exacerbate any natural tendency to procrastinate. If the to-do list contains English homework but it's not due until next Wednesday, it's tempting to leave it until the day before. That might be OK if the do-list were fixed, but

at school it evolves on a daily basis. Leaving work until the last minute routinely yields bunching in the sequencing: when Tuesday rolls around there might be other things which suddenly seem more urgent than the English.
- **inefficiency:** an effective work rhythm is one that sets a steady, sustainable pace. It's a bit like traffic control: we all know that bunching on a motorway is bad news. Traffic moves much more efficiently if there is minimal stopping and starting and a steady pace is maintained. Thinking about the to-do list and then deciding when to do it creates a rhythm that's erratic; it doesn't invite a student to work steadily by thinking about how they can make the best use of the time available to them *now*.

At KS4, your child is unlikely to thank you for micro-managing how they are doing their homework and – even if they did – it would take away the opportunity for them to develop their skills in working independently. It's not really for the parent to be deep in the detail of instructions on homework platforms, or checking their child's answers, but you can make a really constructive difference to your child's working rhythm if you help them decide *when* they'll be working and support them in sticking to their start and stopping points.

Doing this will help your child take stock of the time available and decide which time is best for homework. It helps them check that extracurricular commitments aren't overloading their schedules. It establishes clear boundaries about when mobile phones go away and makes it easier to create suitable, undistracted physical space to get homework done. It creates a straightforward framework where you know when to remind them to get started and when to check in at the end, take an interest in what they've done and say *well done*.

In essence, it sets the end-points, which helps effort feel manageable. It uses the principle of establishing clear finish lines on a daily basis and – as Chapter 5 discussed in more detail – this is a central ingredient for maintaining healthy and constructive levels of engagement.

> **Y12 Student:** *During GCSEs, you can't really do the things that reduce your stress because you have to focus on revising – like you want to take a moment to relax but you can't do that because you should be using that time for revision. There's no way of freeing yourself of that stress. You have to dedicate your time to the exams.*
>
> - Does your child have a clear sense of when it is OK to stop and relax?
> - Are there clear boundaries in place that help your child know when to start and when to finish?
> - If these aren't in place for routine homework, will it be harder for your child to find healthy work habits during more stressful revision periods?

★ Questions to help your child plan a work schedule

Here are the questions that will help you decide a suitable rhythm with your child. It's really constructive for them to take the lead on this; if you listen to them first, it's much more likely that you'll end up with a set of expectations that are fulfillable. In addition, if you do feel it's necessary to disagree, then your child will find it much easier to listen to you if they know that you've taken their view seriously first (see further, Chapter 4).

1. *Let's map out a week-planner.* What time do you get home every day?
2. *What time do you think you should be in bed?* You'll need to do a screen switch-off and hand in your phone a bit before that – what time shall we say for this? Are there other times when you think it would be good to put your phone out of reach?
3. *How much time do you need to relax?* When do you need it most? Is it when you get home or would you rather get homework done first so the rest of the evening is clear after that? Is this the same each day or are some days more draining than others?
4. *What time does this leave you for schoolwork?* Which times on which days? Do you think that's about right? If not, do we need to shift something elsewhere – is the quantity of extracurricular too much?

5. *How would you like me to support you in sticking to this?* Would you like me to remind you to get started or are you confident that you'll stick to this schedule? Shall I check in with you at the end so that homework doesn't spill over and take too much time away from the other things that matter too?

★ What happens if your child wants to do less work than you think is appropriate?

As discussed in Chapter 5, if your child is very disengaged, they may want to do far less work than you think they should. Agreeing with what they offer can feel like you're giving them permission to *not bother*; many parents struggle with this. But it might be worth going back to the material on p106 in Chapter 5: if you want your child to increase their efforts, it's not going to work if you devalue their first offer of what they think they can produce.

If you're trying to help your child change their habits, you need to be realistic that these changes will happen in small steps. Asking for more than your child is ready to give is only going to leave you and them stuck in the gulf of frustration, feeling disappointed that your expectations don't match up. But if you value the beginnings of a change and support your child's offer for the fixed and regular times they'll be working, it's much more likely that, over time, you'll see progress beyond these.

★ What happens if your child feels that they won't get everything done?

Our education system is built around time-capped exams. Setting clear boundaries around when homework starts and when it stops will help your child learn how to fit a task to the time available. Some children find this easier than others. If your child is finding it difficult to finish their homework within an appropriate amount of time, it may be worth going back to the advice in Chapter 5 about the importance of *getting it done* rather than *getting all of it right*. It may also be useful to contact your child's teachers to let them know that your child is spending longer on homework than is manageable within a healthy, balanced schedule. Advice from their teacher will help your child understand what to prioritise within a task so that it's possible to move through it within a suitable amount of time.

★ Avoiding the risk that your child over-promises

There is one risk, though, if your child takes the lead in planning their schedule: children usually want to please the adults they care about. Every time I've talked through a time plan with a student, they've been prone to be over-optimistic about how much work they can do. This can also be true for the disengaged students who – in their heart of hearts – do want things to be different. In adolescence, teenagers want to be taller, stronger, faster than they were: they find it hard to define themselves as able to manage *less* work than they'd like.

The problem with over-promising is that your child may not deliver on their plan and this means that they won't get the motivational boost of meeting the expectations that they've set for themself. So I've got one more piece of advice: when you're helping your child plan their work schedule, remind them that the most effective systems embed a bit of slack and flexibility. *You reckon that you'll do 2 hours after football training on Saturday? That sounds great – but you might be tired and we want to make sure that this rhythm is sustainable and straightforward to achieve. Do you want to do a trial run for the first week where you do 1.5 hours with a break in the middle and see how that goes first? Remember, you can adjust the plan once you've settled into it and know how it feels.*

Serious concerns about well-being

The chances are high that there will be someone in your child's class for whom GCSEs turn out to be a really difficult experience. For some of these children, this will have a significant physical and psychological impact. In addition, for a smaller number of children, serious psychological illnesses can develop during adolescence such as anorexia, OCD or acute anxiety: exam stress may have no causal role in this at all, but the presence of GCSEs can make the recovery process more complicated.

★ Finding help sooner rather than later

It is a difficult truth that sometimes a parent can only do so much. Sometimes teenagers find it much easier to take advice from adults who aren't their parents. Sometimes they find it easier to open up to someone who is not so interconnected with their daily life. It is much more straightforward, however, to work through small problems than big ones. If things are going seriously off-track for your child, the earlier you act on this and bring others in to help, the better.

It's easier said than done, though, because the beginnings of a serious concern are much harder to see because they are smaller and less obviously concerning. So, here's a list of things that it's worth keeping an eye on; if the *yes*-answers start to increase, please reach out to your child's school or GP to discuss further. The list is not exhaustive, and please remember that I'm a teacher, not a doctor or a psychotherapist, but I hope it will be helpful as an indicator of the different types of things to be alert to.

- Do you think your child is hiding things from you to an increasing degree?
- Does your child refuse to talk about school altogether?
- Is your child asking for increasing amounts of time off from school?
- Is your child very resistant to limits around their phone use?
- Does your child refuse to go to bed or routinely stay up late and then find it hard to get up in the morning?
- Does your child seem increasingly withdrawn, listless or despondent about multiple aspects of their life?
- Does your child seem increasingly angry, restless or agitated?
- Have your child's eating habits changed? Have they started to skip breakfast or tell you that they're not hungry because they ate something on the way home?
- Is your child spending longer and longer away from the house?
- Are there physical signs that their experience is becoming more unmanageable? Do they have frequent headaches or stomach

aches? Are they suffering more often from low-level viruses? Are they finding it hard to get to sleep?
- Does your child show increasing signs of compulsive behaviour such as washing their hands in a fixed way, or insisting that their room has to be arranged in a particular order or that they have to do things at a certain time?
- Does your child speak about their life in a way that seems increasingly exaggerated or unbalanced?

School staff, mental health professionals and GPs have the benefit of seeing your child in the context of what is typical at this stage; they'll help you get a sense of whether your concerns are well-founded and they'll be able to advise you on where to go next to get help.

> **Student:** *Where do you draw the line of you not being OK? Especially where there are lots of people who are struggling. It becomes normalised – people saying, 'Yeah I self-harm but lots of people are doing it so it's not that bad.'*
>
> - Would it be easy for your child to initiate a conversation about something really serious? What would the barriers be? You may find it helpful to refer back to the material in Chapter 4, p79.

It's worth remembering that many children do not want their parents to worry about them: as discussed in Chapter 4, they do not want their parents' reaction to make the situation bigger and into something that feels less controlled or manageable. They often don't want the implication that your worry equates to a belief that they're getting something wrong. This means that they may be very resistant – or angry – when you express your concerns.

Bringing someone else in can help with this: *I can see you're angry with me and you think I'm wrong and making a fuss about nothing. Maybe I am. I think the best thing to do is for us to take this to someone who knows more than I do. They can tell me if I'm overreacting, and then I'll know to back off. Doesn't that sound like the best route through? I know you'd rather I take your word for it, but I hope you understand why I think it's sensible just to check it out with someone who has a wider understanding of what's typical in this situation than either you or I do. For you and for me, it's our first time experiencing this; this can make it hard to make the right judgement calls.*

> **Student:** *If they could listen, stay calm and not react more than that, that would be ideal. What's scary is the feeling of changing the whole dynamic, everyone then walking on eggshells, reacting differently to me.*
>
> Acknowledging a serious problem can be very frightening for a teenager; if an adult stays calm, it often helps the situation feel safer. If you are worried about your child and you reach out to a professional, would it help you handle the situation with your child more calmly?

> **KEY IDEAS**
> - KS4 is dominated by the prospect of GCSEs.
> - If your child's predicted grades do not match your expectations, your child will probably notice your disappointment. This will shape their sense of whether they are doing well enough and this may have a negative impact on how they work.
> - Thinking about a margin of tolerance – i.e. the range of results that would still be OK – helps reduce the fear of things going wrong on results day; for most students, this makes it easier to stay motivated and work effectively.
> - Conversations at home can help counterbalance the exam-focused messaging at school; your child may need to be reminded that school is not the only way to measure value.
> - Deciding a clear framework for when your child will start and stop working will help embed steady, manageable work habits.
> - **If you have concerns about your child's physical or mental well-being, it is important to act early and seek professional help.**

CHAPTER 10

Revising effectively for GCSEs; tutoring

Senior Leader (Pastoral): *It's like an arms race for the best grades. We are a big comprehensive school and a large proportion of our students come from aspirational middle-class families.*

This chapter focuses on how to combine aspiration with the realism needed to create a healthy, balanced relationship with revision. You'll find ideas for how you can support your child's revision planning and how you can help your child feel motivated and confident that their revision decisions are sensible. I'll be offering ways to help you work out whether they're doing enough work and I'll be exploring whether or not tutoring is likely to be a good idea. At the end of the chapter, you'll find material about how to motivate your child in the final stages of Y11.

Deciding the revision plan

In Chapter 5, I introduced the idea that if you help your child maintain a scheduled, boundaried relationship with homework, this will make it easier for them to plan their revision. This is true: a child who has a steady rhythm established for homework will be able to make much better decisions about when they can work and when they should stop. If your child can create a realistic schedule for when they'll be revising – and stick to this – then the revision process will feel much smoother, steadier and more reliably productive.

The decisions about *how* to revise within that scheduled time, however, are much more complex than the decisions about how to get homework done. Let's explore why.

The difficulties in deciding how to revise

Deciding what to revise in the time available and how to do it is difficult for the following reasons:

- **number of exams:** 8 or more subjects, 2 or 3 papers a subject? When your child is allocating their available time, they'll have a large number of exams to think about.
- **range of resources:** my generation was limited in how to revise – we had our notes, maybe a textbook, possibly some practice questions if our teachers were particularly industrious. Today's KS4 students have notes, revision guides, lesson PowerPoints, links to different websites, online learning tools, seemingly limitless self-teach videos on YouTube, past papers, mark schemes, examiners' reports. The choice about *what* to revise from has become much more complicated.
- **choosing what to deprioritise:** making a plan is always a matter of choosing *this* over *that* and your child may need support in working out what to cut back if their to-do list is too big for the time available.

The potential difficulty in making revision decisions can lead to one of the following problematic consequences:

- **procrastination or disengagement:** if a child feels overwhelmed by deciding what to do first, they won't get started
- **hyper-engagement:** if a child is naturally hard-working, it can feel easier to try to get *everything* done rather than grapple with the decision of what to prioritise and deprioritise (see further, p94).

Overall, this means that it's much more important for your child to get on and make some decisions than it is to spend ages worrying about whether or not the decisions are the 'right' ones. The golden rule, therefore, as a parent is this: **I'd encourage you to be wary about adding complexity to the decision-making process**. If you second-guess your child's decisions too much, you increase the risk of disengagement or hyper-engagement: neither of these is healthy or constructive.

Resources and revision methods

You might be expecting this chapter to have a long section on the pros and cons of different revision resources and methods. In fact, there isn't one. This is because your child's teachers will be giving them advice. If I were to add an extra layer of complexity to this by recommending one method over another, it wouldn't necessarily help your child.

If your child is familiar and comfortable with using a particular revision method, I'd encourage you to think twice before rocking the boat by suggesting something else. If your child doesn't seem to know how to revise, the best advice will come from their teachers: they will know what is most compatible with the approaches in class and what is likely to work best alongside the main resources available to your child. I will, however, highlight three key principles:

- **Boundaried, tangible, fixed resources** – such as revision guides – tend to be easier to use than material scattered across different platforms or websites. This is because it's easier for a teenager to plan their route through revision if the overall shape of the syllabus is easy to see. A hard-copy revision guide looks the same every time and the start and finish points for each section can be seen at a glance. All of this makes it much easier to use.
- **Input to output** is a core principle for revision: the first stage of the learning process is *receptive*: the student receives information by listening, reading or watching something. To understand something more deeply, however, a student needs to do something with this that is more *active*: they need to use this information and produce something for themselves. This could be making

revision flash cards for key points, it could be saying material out loud to explain it again in their own words, it could be practice exam questions or online quizzes: the format doesn't matter as much as the basic principle that *producing* something creates the *input to output* mechanism that establishes a much stronger, active engagement with the material.

- **Memorising material is hard work:** it's much easier to familiarise yourself with something (for example, read it and make flash cards) than it is to commit it to memory. Memorising material takes a lot of concentration and most students find they need to do it in small batches and interweave regular breaks into it. It is helpful, therefore, when planning revision to think about the different time allocations for *familiarisation* and *memorisation*: setting short, specific time windows for memorisation will help your child engage with both parts of the process.

★ Thinking through revision decisions

As a parent, you can make a big difference if you support your child through the process of making their decisions. *Support* doesn't mean *make the decisions for them*: your role is not to work out the best game plan for your child. This is partly because – as explained on p155 – you're the parent, not the teacher. It is also because – if you make the decisions for your child – you don't give them the chance to develop important skills in working independently.

Instead, if you're ready to act as a sounding board and listen to your child while they talk through their decisions, you'll make it much easier for your child to feel confident and motivated about their plan. This will make it easier for them to get on with the revision and reduce the risk of problematic procrastination or hyper-engagement. Here are some questions which will help with this:

- ***There may not be enough time to do it all: which subjects need the least time? Tell me why.*** Perhaps counter-intuitively, this question is a more useful opener than *what are you going to prioritise?* It's more useful because it's usually the question that has been thought about least and which is harder to answer, especially if there's a lot of *don't forget about this* at school. For a disengaged, demotivated child, the question helps the process feel more manageable. For a hyper-engaged child, it helps them feel better about the boundaries they are setting. If your child's reasons sound sensible, don't second-guess them: they probably are sensible.

- *Let's imagine you only had half the time available for Biology: what would be your priorities then?* Imagining a plan which fits into half the time creates a starting point that helps the real plan feel more comfortable; it also creates a safety net because if something happens and time is cut short, there's a game plan already in place.
- *Have you thought about what your main revision resource will be for this subject?* Different students revise in different ways, but if your child is keen to flit about from one thing to another, it's worth probing this a bit and checking that the benefit for them is real rather than a way to break the tedium of *here we go again*. As before, though, if their reasons sound considered and sensible, don't second-guess them; if your child can explain the benefit of their chosen approach, it probably means it's working for them.
- *What are you going to do to help make sure you can use the knowledge rather than just revisit it?* Asking this question guards against the risk of sitting fairly passively, scrolling through one 30-second video after another. Writing mind maps, revision cards, doing practice questions, saying things out loud: the method matters far, far less than the need to do *something* with the material.
- *How are you going to memorise the material? Have you divided it up into chunks so you can learn it a bit at a time with enough breaks in between? Would you like me to test you?* Asking questions like these helps to present *memorisation* as something distinct from revisiting or practising material. Offering to test your child also creates the opportunity to celebrate their efforts on the way

through, boosting morale and motivation. **If you do test your child, keep your focus on what has been meaningfully achieved that day and praise them for this, rather than dwelling on their mistakes.** Your child is more likely to be motivated to keep revising if they feel their revision is going well; if they get told by their parents that it's not good enough yet, they're much more likely to disengage.

Whatever the revision plan looks like, you'll help your child stay motivated if you encourage them to see the benefit of what they've managed to complete. If they've been over-optimistic and find themselves behind on their plan, then reassure them that it's natural to have to adjust things as the revision period unfolds.

If your child is finding it hard to make decisions, you may find the *which option is better* technique from Chapter 6 helpful (see further, p121).

> **Student:** *Even though I was so stressed out, I ended up not doing anything. I constantly felt guilty and overwhelmed.*
>
> If revision feels boundaried and manageable, it's much easier to get started. What's going to work better for your child? Telling them that *GCSEs are really important and they need to get their revision right* or helping your child feel that their plans are sensible and well thought through?

★ What to do if your child is worried about revision

Interested, supportive conversations at home about the process of revision – rather than the importance of the results – will help your child feel much better and more motivated about revision. But some children need more reassurance than others, and you may find that your child continues to worry about whether they're doing enough revision or revising in the right way.

It's helpful, therefore, to take an interest in the revision process in the run-up to lower-stakes tests, internal exams or GCSE mocks. It's easier for your child to take ownership of the decision-making process for these tests because the risks are lower. If they are worried that they won't be doing enough or that they *can't leave this out because the teacher said we had to revise it*, then remind them that internal exams are there to practise making choices. If the test result isn't as hoped, it's possible to recalibrate afterwards. Remind your child that they will get better at planning their revision with each cycle: they can experiment now and use this to inform the choices moving forwards.

> **Y13 Student:** *Teacher validation has a massive impact. Sometimes when you get tests back, having 1:1 chats with teachers really helps – having the conversation – this makes a big difference.*
>
> If your child is very anxious about their revision decisions, a 1:1 chat with their teacher may help them feel better. If this is possible at your child's school, could you help them think through what to ask their teacher? Do they need a list of all the things they *could* do, or do they need reassurance that their decisions are sensible about what to deprioritise?

But are they doing enough revision?

What counts as enough? This question becomes more pressing in Y11 because the closer your child gets to GCSEs, the less boundaried their relationship with work can become. It's no longer only a matter of scheduled homework tasks: when it comes to the more shapeless, less structured task of revision, it may feel increasingly difficult to work out what on earth *does* count as enough.

> **Y12 Student:** *Whenever I sat down to relax, there was always a feeling of I could be doing something else, there's another piece of work I could be doing.*
>
> - Have you asked your child if they have a clear idea of what counts as enough revision?
> - If their answer is uncertain or unrealistic, what does this show you about the support they may need from you?

The problems caused by the *is it enough* question

Are they doing enough revision? The problem with this question is that it's difficult to answer *yes*. This is because saying *yes, it's enough* implies that there would be no benefit in working harder. For any individual subject, doing a bit more work may well seem like a good idea; it might move things up to a higher grade. Your child's teachers probably won't want to limit the grade outcomes and the messaging in class may be full of things that the students *could* do if they want to improve their grades.

But your child isn't working on just one subject in isolation; they're balancing that subject against all their other subjects and – ideally – maintaining the sort of work-rest-play balance that keeps their physical and mental health in good shape. The net result is that most Y11 students end up faced with a hypothetical to-do list which is far longer than could ever be completed in the time available. It's no surprise that many students get majorly stressed out by the feeling that they're not going to get enough done.

> **Student:** *In form time we went through how to build a revision timetable, but no one actually talked through the number of hours. There was a sense that each teacher thinks that their subject is the only subject; I found myself listening to the teacher's advice and thinking, yeah, if I just did Geography then I could do all of that, but I don't.*

> Does your child understand that what it's possible to revise in the time available is likely to be different from the totality of all the revision that *could* be done?

Trying to answer the *is it enough* question

Students and parents can find themselves trying to work out what *enough* looks like by using the following metrics:

- how hard other students are working
- how hard someone else in the family is working
- how hard the parents worked in preparation for exams
- looking at school reports to see if there's room for improvement and assuming that if the grades aren't in the top band then *surely a bit more would be better.*

The problem with all of this is that it looks to the sides: it compares your child with someone else and it assumes that if more is available, then it's clearly a good idea. It doesn't help at all with finding the balance that is right for your child: it doesn't factor in their energy levels, their commitments, their priorities or needs. Your child will need to work out a revision schedule which is right for *them*, and this may be different from what would work for someone else.

> **Y12 Student:** *For GCSE revision, everyone has different situations – no people are the same – no people revise the same – this makes it harder to know if you've revised enough. Some people can just do it easily, some people have to go over and over.*
>
> Does your child think that they work more quickly or slowly than others? How does this impact how they feel about revision?

> **Student:** *My advice for GCSEs? Don't compare your revision to other people's revision. It doesn't help if your parents are telling you, 'This person is revising this much, you should be revising the same.'*
>
> • How often do you – or your child – try to work out if something is going OK by making comparisons with others?

★ Better ways to answer the *is it enough* question

If you're trying to work out if your child is doing *enough work for them,* the predicted grades from the school will give you a baseline indication of where things stand: it's reasonable to assume that your child's default effort levels are about right for their predicted grades.

You may still be left, however, with the question of whether *doing more would be better.* If so, I'd encourage you to beware the allure of *if they do more, their grade might be higher.* This may be true enough but it doesn't change the fact that your child still has to set boundaries around how much they work; they still have to make decisions about doing *this*, rather than *that* piece of work. If they are constantly questioning whether *more would be better*, they may end up demoralised by the persistent doubt that their *revision decisions aren't the right ones.*

It's much more constructive to focus on the knowable, controllable aspects of the process, rather than the unknowable, uncertain nature of the outcome. So I'm going to suggest letting go of asking *would more revision make the exam go better* and ask instead whether the work rate is suitable for a healthy and productive rhythm *today*?

As a parent, how about using these questions instead as a way of working out if the revision process is about right?

- Does my child seem clear in their decisions about when to work and for how long?
- Does my child find it straightforward to work at the times they intended, indicating that their rhythm is sustainable?

- Is my child open to reviewing their work plan at suitable intervals, recalibrating if they need to and thinking about the pros *and* cons of doing more or doing less?
- Do I still see my child having fun on a regular basis and doing things they clearly enjoy, indicating that they're maintaining a balance which means that GCSEs are unlikely to grind them down?
- Is my child developing their skills in explaining which bits of work they are prioritising and why? If they don't manage to finish everything they'd hoped to do today, are they calm and reflective about how to adapt their plan for tomorrow?
- Does my child recognise the benefit of the individual bits of work they are doing, or do they seem demoralised, saying *there's no point revising, it's not going to make any difference*?
- Does my child sound reasonably calm about their to-do list or do they keep saying *I've got too much to do, I'll never get it all done*?

If these questions throw up areas of concern, then it might be worth going back to the material in Chapters 5 and 9. In Chapter 5 you'll find advice about how to motivate your child to engage better with schoolwork; on p180 in Chapter 9 you'll find guidance on how to help your child think through their time plans.

> **Student:** *The biggest thing that helps is having a really set work-life balance, e.g. saying at 6pm onwards I'm stopping. This really helps you not feel guilty about not working. Having something that isn't exams is really important. Being about to clock off is really helpful.*
>
> Many schools suggest using the school timetable as a framework for a revision timetable during the holidays: what are the benefits to keeping revision within limited and scheduled time windows?

Does my child need a tutor?

Tutoring has become big business. Getting a tutor has become an educational snowball, rolling along and getting bigger and bigger through its own momentum. So many teenagers get tutors that it seems to have become the go-to solution: *not going as well as you'd hoped? Get a tutor.* It's become so ubiquitous that as a parent it's possible to end up feeling guilty if you're not booking tutoring: if everyone else is talking about the tutors they've bagged for their children, are you somehow remiss for not providing this additional boost?

Tutoring has its benefits: one-to-one help allows a child to go at the pace that suits them, ask as many questions as they like, and do tasks specifically designed for their needs. For students who have missed a lot of school, are lacking in confidence, or find it difficult to engage in a large-class setting, tutoring can be transformative. But just because it's transformative in some circumstances, it doesn't mean it's equally useful in all circumstances. As I'm about to explain, tutoring is not necessarily the educational silver bullet that it seems.

Does tutoring always improve things?

The first thing to understand is that one-to-one teaching is much harder to get right than it looks. On a surface level, it seems easier. Class control? Not an issue. Achieving an atmosphere that feels purposeful, focused *and* pleasant? Much more straightforward if you're tutoring and can combine science explanations with a friendly chat, a cup of tea and some biscuits.

The bit that's much harder isn't the *teaching*, it's the *learning*, and the reason for this is that in a teacher-pupil interaction there's an unavoidable pie chart for who's doing something effortful. Unless the teacher is unusually skilled, the more the teacher does, the more the student sits back and does *less*. Let's pause on this because although it's obvious once you think about it, it often isn't noticed.

Tutoring can be ineffective for all sorts of reasons, but the biggest of these is that – as a one-to-one tutor – it's very hard to pull back enough for the student to do *more*, not *less*. Asking more of the student and offering less of your teaching can feel like you're not earning your keep. It's also much harder because you don't know the ins and outs of what the child has done at school; as a tutor, you end up asking questions like *has your teacher explained surds to you yet?* The most likely answer is *sort of but not really* and what happens then is the tutor begins to reteach it.

Yes, that's what we're paying for. Are you though? Are you aiming to double up on the teaching or are you aiming to boost your child's learning? If you're aiming to boost your child's learning, what you really need to achieve is more *doing* from your child and less sitting back, sort-of-listening while someone else is busy doing all the doing.

All this means that it's very easy for the tutoring to happen, for your child to say it's useful because they're left with neat folders of additional resources and different explanations, for the tutor to feel like they've made a difference because they've really given a lot to your child, but for the learning outcomes to be either no better or even a bit worse. *A bit worse? How can that be?* Let me explain.

Common pitfalls in tutoring

The risk that your child is getting more *listening* but not much more *doing* isn't the only pitfall of tutoring. Here are some more:

- **It's OK, I've got a tutor.** Teenagers believe that a tutor will help them. That's good for motivation, but it's not always good for their engagement in class. It's not uncommon in today's classroom to see a teenager zone out, call them back in by reminding them to focus and hear them say *don't worry – I'll go over it with my tutor later.* Tutoring can create the risk that a student disengages further in class in the false belief that their tutor will achieve everything in one hour that would otherwise have needed roughly three times as long to deliver in routine lessons.
- **A distorted picture:** does your child's teacher know they've got a tutor? Tutors often help students with their homework. There's a benefit to this in so far as the student does at least get

the homework done, but the risk is that they hand in homework that is better than they'd have managed on their own. This is problematic because it distorts the picture: this impacts what happens in class, the questions that the teacher directs at your child and the advice that they get given.
- **Less exam-ready:** doing homework with a tutor also means that when your child is sitting in the exam – without their tutor – they're *less* practised for the experience of working it out on their own than they would have been if they'd been doing all their homework independently.
- **More complexity:** think about that nice folder of extra resources. The end result is that the child has *more* resources to revise from and – as discussed above – this adds complexity. In teaching, consistency is key: if you're explaining something, it's much better to use the same words every time so that there's a stable set of knowledge which is much easier to remember. If your tutor is reteaching everything, your child has to listen to two versions concurrently. Every time there's a small difference in how something has been explained, the risk increases that your child is left with a muddier, more muddled understanding.
- **Burden on time:** the time spent with a tutor is time taken away from something else and it's important to be sure that the swap is a net gain rather than a net loss. I've taught teenagers who are falling asleep in class: *You'd better have an early night*, I say. *I can't, Miss. I've got two hours of tutoring and then all my other homework to do.* If adding in tutoring tips the balance into *too tired overall*, it's going to make things harder, not easier.

Physics Lead: *Loads of students have tutors now. The relationship between tutor and child is a financial one: the tutor wants the child to feel like it's going well. The tutor will sit through a hard question with them. The child hasn't gone through the struggle for themselves. Not*

> being familiar with the struggle means that you get to the exam and you think, 'I don't know what this means'. They haven't learned how to get through it on their own.
>
> In the extract above, a Physics teacher describes one of the downsides of tutor-dependency. When a child has to sit and have a go at a question on their own, what skills do they learn even if they get the answer wrong?

★ How to make sure that tutoring is effective

As I mentioned earlier, there are times when tutoring really is a good idea: if there have been gaps in the teaching because of staff absence or because your child has missed school, for example, or if your child is so demoralised that they'll get a big boost from an hour a week where there's one-to-one attention. But it's still worth making sure that this tutoring is effective and so if you do sign up for tutoring, it may be helpful to keep the following principles in mind.

- **Consult your child's teacher:** if you're thinking about a tutor, it's worth asking your child's teacher if they think it would be a good idea. If their response is *yes – what your child most needs to do is sit down and learn this vocabulary* then their advice will create useful parameters for what you ask the tutor to do.
- **Keep the connection to classwork tight:** tutoring needs to support core classroom business, not replace it, so ask your child which bits of the syllabus they need help with. Make sure they find the resources their teacher has given them for this topic so that these resources can be used by the tutor, whether or not the tutor would have done things the same way.
- **Be wary of reteaching:** it's much better for the student if the tutor asks them to use their class notes and teach back to the tutor what they can understand from these resources. Doing it this way is slower in the short term – and a bit harder for the tutor – but

it is far more effective in the long term. It turns the child into the *doer* and it increases their familiarity with their class material. It maintains the consistency of the phrasing that their teacher has used – and will use again – in class. It makes it more likely that the student will engage better in class.

- **Listen for silence:** if your tutor is talking most of the time, this is not good news. If they're jumping in too soon to help your child do their homework, this is also not good news. Helping too soon creates tutor-dependency, it doesn't build independent understanding. Ask your tutor their strategies for making sure that the child does enough on their own in their presence. If the tutor looks blank, then think twice. If the tutor says something like *yes, this is central – I use the 5-minute timer method – I make sure my tutee works on their own for at least 5 minutes at a time before asking for help, I answer questions at the start and at the end but I don't distract in the middle*, then you're in business.
- **Ask your child to show you what *they* have done afterwards:** if at the end of a session your child has sheets with their tutor's handwriting on, not theirs, this is no good. Tell your child that the tutoring should be a vehicle for them to do more, not to watch while their tutor beavers away. Ask your child which piece of work they'll be doing that session and then ask them to tell you at the end which bits they did on their own. Delight in the bits that they *didn't* need the tutor for and ask them which bits they think they *won't* need the tutor for next time.

The end of Y11: Keeping going

It's a marathon, not a sprint. Many people describe GCSEs in this way. If you've done any endurance fitness events, you'll know that the hardest section is often around about the two-thirds mark. You're tired, you need to keep going, but the finish line is still a long way off.

When your child is in Y11, they may feel this way for much of the year, especially if they have to do two sets of mock exams before the real thing. As a parent, it's useful to think about how you can help keep going through the hard yards of *I wish it were over but it really isn't*.

I still remember one of the first Y11 workshops I did as a visiting speaker. The school had invited me to talk to the students about exam stress. Whole year group sessions are often a tough gig: connecting with the students is tricky when there are so many of them, they're often a bit jaded about yet another life-advice session from some random stranger, and there are usually only a few who are willing to put their hands up to answer a question. We were about 20 minutes into the 1-hour event and we were focusing on a healthy and sustainable route through Y11. *I'm doing a session for your parents after school*, I said, *so tell me: what would you like them to hear about how to support you best?*

The room changed; hands shot up. Here are some of the things that they said:

- *They don't need to keep telling me I've got GCSEs; I know I do.*
- *If I come home after a disappointing test result, I don't want my mum to go into solutions mode, telling me what I need to do to fix it. I'm already disappointed, I know what to do, I just want a bit of space.*
- *They need to understand that sometimes all the revision and past papers make me really bored and frustrated. If I get grumpy at home, I don't mean to behave badly, but sometimes I can't manage anything else.*
- *It's the small things that help – a cup of tea, coming into my room to give me a hug, that sort of thing.*
- *I'm really, really tired and I'm already trying my best, even if they don't think I am.*

Then I asked them a different question: *do your parents know this?* The room changed again. If you've been teaching as long as I have, you learn to recognise when the answer is, collectively, *no*. I paused, then asked, *so why don't you tell them?*

When I told this story at the parents' event later the same day, an affectionate chuckle went round the room. *But I could ask you the same question*, I said. *Have you asked your child what helps and what doesn't?* Once again, the atmosphere shifted and a collective *no* hung in the air.

★ **Asking your child what would help**
Parenting habits are formed when children are young. You don't get to discuss parenting methods directly with your baby or toddler. But a teenager is different. So why not sit down and ask your child directly what would help them get through the slog? If you ask them when they're calm and have the headspace to think, you might be surprised at how useful their advice is.

> **Y10 student:** *Sometimes it's hard to work out what would help but you definitely know what doesn't. If parents are willing to hear this then it'd help them stop doing the things that their children find really difficult.*
>
> - Do you think it's straightforward for your child to tell you if there's something they think you need to do differently? Is it straightforward for you to hear this?
> - When does this sort of conversation go best? In the middle of a row when everyone's already upset, or at a time when everyone's feeling calm and able to listen?

Incentivising the final push

Establishing a healthy day-to-day rhythm, maintaining a balanced perspective, supporting the decision process about what to prioritise and why: all of this matters throughout KS4. But towards the end, many parents find themselves tempted to facilitate a sprint finish to the marathon.

Do you think you'll offer an incentive for results? Will you offer to pay out for particular grades? Many parents do and many teenagers like the idea of cashing in on results day. When I think back to my own GCSEs, I can remember the ripples around my class as we heard what other people were getting as payouts for different grades.

My parents refused to do this. As a 16-year-old, I didn't appreciate this. I remember doing the sums about the sorts of cash I'd rack up if only I'd had someone else's parents instead. I tried to argue the toss – probably quite petulantly – but my parents were steadfast. *Don't make the mistake of thinking that an A is £10 better than a B*, they said. *We're interested in how you prepare, not what you get.*

With all the indignant arrogance of a 16-year-old, I thought that on this one, my parents' argument was fatuous. *Of course an A grade is more valuable than a B*, I thought, flouncing off to my bedroom, *that's why it's more impressive on a UCAS form.* I was right about the UCAS form, but this didn't mean my parents were wrong. For a high-ranking university, an A is more valuable than a B. They want the students with the A grades. The B-grade students are worth less to them. But I see now why my parents were right: they were not a university, they were my parents. I was their child, not a CV in a selection pile. Was I worth less to them with a B grade than I would have been with an A grade if – all the while – I'd demonstrated the characteristics they cared most about, such as reliability, honesty and sensible decision-making?

★ Valuing the grades or the process?

Incentives and consequences – parenting is often a delicate dance around these different steps. By the end of Y11 your child will almost certainly be bored, tired and heartily sick of it all. I'm all for incentivising the final push, though there are plenty of ways of doing this which don't involve money. But whatever you use as an incentive, there's still a choice about what you incentivise: is it the outcome or the process?

Does the incentive materialise in August, dependent on the grade and all the external variables that accompany this? Or can it be earned in the here and now, based on the way that your child works? Is the incentive more motivating if it's in the far-off hinterland of the post-GCSE summer holiday, or would it be better to unleash its boost week by week as a way for your child to feel the benefit of staying accountable to the plans they have made? And – if you're still tempted to set a price on results and pay out in cash when August rolls around – maybe think about this: on results day, do you really want your child to feel that their worth to you, as their parents, is £50 less than if they'd done as well as their friend?

KEY IDEAS

- Making decisions about revision can be difficult: you can support your child by listening to their thoughts about what to do next and reassuring them that their reasons sound sensible. If your child is too worried about whether their decisions are 'right', it will be much harder for them to make any decisions at all. This will have a negative impact on how effectively they work.
- Many teenagers – and their parents – worry that they are not doing enough work; you can support your child by helping them establish a daily rhythm that is sensible and sustainable.
- Tutoring can be transformative, but it does not always benefit the child; if you want tutoring to be effective, it needs to connect directly with what is happening in class and – during each session – your child needs to be working harder than the tutor.
- As KS4 progresses, your child will know what they find helpful and supportive; it's worth asking them what this is.
- In the final stages of Y11, if you're keen to offer incentives, it's more constructive to incentivise the process than the outcome.

CHAPTER 11

Starting sixth form

Head of Sixth Form College: *We run around at Y11, put interventions in left, right and centre and then 12 weeks later they rock up in a pair of jeans and we expect them to be independent.*

When teenagers start sixth form, their school habits have been formed through their experiences in KS3 and KS4. At the start of Y12, their most recent school experience is the end of Y11. They arrive with one set of habits but they'll need to adjust these to the new expectations of the sixth form environment. This chapter will explore how you can support them in this so that they're ready to develop their skills and approaches as they move through KS5.

Letting go of Y11

Let's repeat the statement from the paragraph above: at the start of Y12, a teenager's most recent school experience is the end of Y11. Does this seem trivially true? It's true, but not trivial because the end of Y11 is bizarrely atypical in the educational journey; there's often a sharp contrast between how school felt then and how it's going to feel now in the fresh new world of sixth form.

I use the word *journey* because it implies being on the move. In education you should be on the move, progressing from one thing to something new and then something new again. The end of Y11 is like being stuck in a loop; it's a *Groundhog Day* set of repeating actions. Here's a practice question, here's another one, here's another one. Let's revisit something that you've already done several times over (see further, Chapter 3). It's an effective way of getting good grades because it reduces the risk of problematic exam-day surprises, but it also means that at the end of Y11, there's very little that's new or unfamiliar.

This means that the fast pace of lots of new material at the start of Y12 can take students by surprise. What's more, it's not just the pace or the newness of lesson content that's different: the whole process of learning changes in the sixth form. Teenagers are usually ready for more relaxed uniform requirements, they know their timetable will be different, they're probably looking forward to *no more French* or *Physics* or whatever it was that they liked least at GCSE, but they may not be ready for how different the classroom experience will be in a Key Stage built around a greater degree of independence and a more sophisticated, mature way of thinking.

So, if you want to help your child adjust to Y12, you may need to encourage them to think about two different things:

1. What their Y11 habits were and why they need to let go of them
2. How and why Y12 is going to be different.

Let's look at each of these now.

The Y11 habits

As Chapter 3 explained, in order to get good results at GCSE, schools have to teach students to do exactly what the test requires. Mark schemes are really prescriptive: if a child doesn't know exactly how a particular type of question will be marked, they'll end up missing out on marks, even if they know and understand the subject content really well.

Many teachers believe that the most efficient way to teach to the test is to tell the students how to answer a question in advance. The theory behind this is that getting it wrong creates inefficiency: it sets up a bad habit that then needs to be corrected with additional practice. There's also the risk that getting it wrong demoralises the students and they disengage. On this view, it seems a no-brainer: give front-loaded instructions so that students have the best chance of getting it right each time.

In the classroom, time is limited and teachers want their classes to do well. If you watched one of my Y11 lessons, you'd see me teaching to the test via very direct instructions too. But if I'm thinking about education in its purest sense, I'd tell you that – although it gets good grades at GCSE – there's a whopping downside to all this. This method of teaching is extremely mistake averse and it reduces the opportunity for students to learn how to think more independently or build confidence in their ability to make a sensible decision on their own. It doesn't create much opportunity for students to develop the skills they'll need for the more demanding, more independent sixth form courses. At the end of Y11, it's usually the case that students know how to answer a question before they start and they've been trained to wait for instructions rather than think for themselves.

> **Head of Chemistry:** *Some students focus on learning a particular method – they focus on routine expertise – this is the way I solve that particular problem. They then fall apart if they get something different – they don't have any flexible, adaptable thinking.*
>
> If you asked your child whether they had a choice about how to answer a question in Y11, what would they say? How is this likely to affect their ability to work more independently in the sixth form or respond to questions that may be more complex and less predictable?

Why is KS5 different?

I've already said that in the sixth form, the pace of learning will be faster. This is true, but I doubt it's taken you by surprise. In addition, the lesson content will be more challenging; this probably isn't surprising either.

But the differences between KS5 and KS4 go much deeper than the pace and challenge of the new material, so it's worth pausing to consider what these differences are and why, educationally, this is the case.

Formal education is a journey that's designed to stop: at the end, students leave, independently, to get on with their adult lives. In theory, they should have acquired the following skills:

- the ability to learn things without needing a teacher
- the confidence to deal with new, unfamiliar situations
- mature thought patterns which enable them to avoid blunt, inaccurate generalisations (see further, Chapter 6).

Educationally and developmentally, the gear shift in KS5 is a good thing because it suits what the adolescent brain needs at that age. Professor Sarah-Jayne Blakemore is one of Britain's leading neuroscientific researchers into adolescent brain development. Her award-winning book, *Inventing Ourselves*, outlines the research that evidences how – during adolescence – the human brain develops its capacity for independence, allowing a teenager to become increasingly alert to their own opinions and values, distinguishing these from the opinions of others. In adolescence, teenagers experiment with different approaches; they unlock a creativity that allows them to find new ways of doing things and to think for themselves, rather than just copying what someone else has shown them to do.

I'm wary of generalising too far about sixth form subjects – syllabuses take students deeper into each subject and this means that the differences between them become more pronounced – but if I had to attempt a generalisation, I'd say this: KS5 content provides more opportunity to develop the brain functions that facilitate a more creative, nuanced and independent mode of thinking. KS5 syllabuses offer more opportunity for students to think for themselves, make connections between material and navigate complex, more detailed and more flexible thought sequences.

In order to facilitate this move towards independence, a greater proportion of the pie chart of learning in KS5 falls to the student. The proportions shift between time allocated to lessons and time allocated to independent study: in the sixth form, students are expected to do much more on their own.

Six ways in which KS5 may feel different from GCSEs

It's time for specifics: let's set out a list which details what's likely to be different about Y12. You'll notice that this list isn't subject specific and – because different subjects involve different thought processes – there will be variations in the degree to which each element applies for your child's subject choices.

1. **A shift in the balance between known / not-known:** as new syllabus content is introduced in Y12 – and at a much faster pace than in Y11 – students are likely to feel there's a lot they don't know properly yet. This can create a fairly dramatic shift in the internal barometer that creates the sense of whether they are on top of things or not. If the proportion of not-known material gets too high, there's a risk that the student feels overwhelmed, withdraws and gives up.
2. **Personal opinion rarely feels 'right' in the way that a simple, GCSE answer does:** for subjects where *constructing an argument* is core business, students have to think for themselves to a much greater degree. This is interesting and liberating but it can also feel unsettling and uncertain because there's no longer the security of *the answer is the one I've already been taught.*
3. **Marks will be lower:** content is new, questions are harder and skills have not yet been practised repeatedly. This means that marks will almost certainly be lower than their exam-ready, polished equivalents at the end of Y11.
4. **Tasks are longer:** this is true in an obvious, literal way – essays are longer, a piece of Maths homework will have more questions, vocab lists have more words on them. But it's also often true for the thought sequences: there are more steps to think through before the answer emerges. The important consequence of this is that – at the start of a question – the answer may not

be obvious. The student may have to start trying to work it out and it may take several steps, including several false starts, before things click into place.

5. **More work needs to be done independently:** there will be more homework per subject than there was at KS4. Y12 students need to boost whatever is taught in the classroom with things that they learn independently in their own time. This is very different from Y11, where homework is largely about practising and reinforcing something the teacher taught during a lesson. This means that there is an increased need for students to use their own time in a disciplined, planned and effective way.

6. **There are more decisions to be made about priorities:** the increase in independent study also means that students have to make more decisions about what they'll work on and when, what they'll prioritise and what – for them – counts as enough (see further, p193).

Overall, therefore, the gear-shift from KS4 to KS5 will feel different, unfamiliar and probably much harder than Y11. Many students find this energising, interesting and freeing, but – for a large number of students – the increased level of challenge can bring the risk that it's harder to be motivated and engage in a constructive, confident way (see further, Chapter 5).

> **Assistant Head, Teaching & Learning:** *In educational theory, there is the idea of virtuous and vicious cycles of learning: in a virtuous cycle of learning, doing something that feels easy feels good, you keep doing it. But in a vicious cycle, the harder stuff feels like it's not working, so the students don't want to do it.*
>
> - Does your child feel that Y12 is going *better* than Y11? If the answer is *no*, has it impacted their motivation? Are they finding it harder to get the work done?

★ How you can help your child adapt to Y12

What's your role, then, as a parent? How can you help your child adapt to the different terrain of Y12?

It's probably useful to restate some boundaries around the different roles that students, teachers and parents need to play. The role for parents is not to double up on what teachers are doing, and it's certainly not to take away from what your child needs to do for themselves. Let's summarise:

- **Students** have to get on and do the work that is necessary. There's no way around this; if a student doesn't do the work, the learning won't happen.
- **Teachers** create the route map, deciding which bits of learning are allocated to lessons or independent study; they are there to advise their students on what to do and how to do it.
- **Parents** provide the support which helps their child do the bits that need to be done independently.

Those are the headlines, but here is the detail: as a parent, you definitely don't need to give advice on how to write an essay or what a good answer looks like; you don't need to know the fine details of syllabus requirements or assessment objectives. Instead, you can support your child in the following ways:

- take an interest in their decisions about when to work, when to stop and what to prioritise within this time
- help them think about how to adapt to the new environment of Y12
- listen and empathise when they're finding something difficult or stressful
- offer the counterbalance that helps them maintain a healthy perspective (see further, p39 and p173).

To help you do this, there are two key strategies you can use: you can help your child create a healthy study routine at home and you can talk to them about school in a way that will help them think about and manage the new process of learning which Y12 will throw at them.

★ **Strategy #1: Establishing a healthy study routine**
A healthy study routine is one that is planned and sustainable. Making and delivering on a plan helps a teenager feel confident and on top of what they are doing, but it's important that the plan is realistic and manageable in the time available.

Planning can get harder at KS5 because work is more open-ended and it can be harder for a student to work out what counts as enough (see further, p193). The principles for how to support your child in this are the same as they were at KS4. You may find it useful to go back to the material in Chapters 9 and 10, and the general overview given in Chapter 5. In particular, you may find the following material helpful:

- the importance of setting achievable finish lines – p101
- getting homework done, rather than getting it all right – p103
- getting the cost:benefit ratio right for effort – p106
- creating space for your child to offload if they are demoralised, angry, worried or stressed – p108
- questions to help your child decide their study routine – p180.

The principles work equally well at KS5 and KS4, but there are two new things to have in mind that are specific to the KS5 context:

1. As teenagers get older, their circadian rhythm often drives them to stay up later and later, but working late into the night is rarely a good plan. This is particularly relevant if someone is feeling stressed or overwhelmed. If your child is upset but says they have to keep working, encourage them to head to bed, reset and start again with fresher eyes the next day.

2. At KS5, your child may be much less interested in discussing their work with you. If so, this is a natural consequence of their increasing independence, but it doesn't make the offer of support redundant. It still makes a difference to a teenager to know that their parent is available, interested and ready to listen.

> **Y13 Student:** *What helps? Just someone being there – especially my mum – she doesn't understand how A levels work, it's not like she can help me with Chemistry, but she's there and if I want to talk about it, she'll listen. She's said that she won't judge me about whether I'm doing enough or not and that's really helpful.*
>
> How often do you offer to listen to your child in case they'd like to talk?
>
> Do you remind your child that you're happy to be a sounding board if they want to think something through? Or do they feel that if they start talking, you'll start telling them what to do? (See further, Chapter 4.)

★ Strategy #2: Talking about school

If you want to help your child adjust to the new process of learning at KS5, there are seven key principles that are useful for them to have in mind.

I'm summarising them here so that they are all in one place, but on p218 you'll find some sample conversation sequences which exemplify how they can be used in everyday conversations.

1. **Something is better than nothing:** this is very obviously true, but it can be hard to believe in the value of *something* if – at the same time – it feels *not yet good enough*. At the start of Y12, it's very hard to get everything right; your child may be faced with a piece of work that they think they're about to get *all wrong* and

they'll need to remember that it's much better to do *something* than nothing at all. This principle will also be important later on for longer pieces of work, such as coursework: if your child doesn't prioritise getting *something* done, there's a risk of falling behind with deadlines, making the overall task more stressful and much harder.

2. **Headlines matter as much as the detail:** GCSE trains students to focus on tiny bits of detail; for the bigger syllabuses at KS5, your child will need to combine detail with a clear overview of headline content. Knowing the headlines makes it easier to anchor detail in place, making the detail less overwhelming. Knowing the headlines also helps a student see connections between different parts of a syllabus; this helps them work in a more sophisticated way.

3. **Marks need to be interpreted differently in the new context of Y12:** your child may need your help to remember that 60% in Y12 might be better than 85% in Y11 even though, on the surface, it doesn't look like it.

4. **The first step might not be familiar:** sixth form work is full of more complex tasks involving multiple steps. At GCSE, tasks are much shorter and front-loaded instructions mean that your child may be used to seeing the finishing line from the starting position. In the sixth form, your child may need to learn to be much more experimental in their approach, trying one thing, then another, jiggling various keys in the lock until something clicks. They'll need to learn to see this experimentation as an important part of the process, not as evidence that they are in some way failing because they couldn't get it right straightaway.

5. **You don't have to think what someone else thinks:** this principle applies in the classroom and more generally. At GCSE, it's best not to question the teacher: this is because GCSE mark schemes don't leave much room for negotiation.

At KS5, there'll be more tasks where personal opinion matters. Beyond the classroom, at KS5 students need to make more decisions for themselves, both about their own independent studying and about the direction they'd like their life to take. This means that they'll need to take a much more sceptical, questioning approach to what they hear other people say so that there's room for them to work out what they think is right for them.

6. **Effective prioritisation becomes increasingly important and individual:** sixth form qualifications have bigger syllabuses which need to be navigated within the same time limits and – as students get older – there are more demands on their time. Part-time jobs, more responsibility within the home, socialising, extracurricular interests: these all mean that individual students have rhythms to their week which may vary considerably from others in their year group. For many students, this means that they'll need to make more decisions about what they will – and won't – give their time to.

7. **It doesn't have to be enjoyable to be worthwhile:** this one probably sounds a bit bleak and, if your child is fizzing with academic excitement you may not need it, but I'd say that 99.99% of the students I've taught have found some aspects of their KS5 courses to be more of a slog than a joy. That's not because there's anything fundamentally wrong with sixth form syllabuses; it's the natural result of teenagers growing into their own sense of self. As teenagers become more individual and aware of their own interests, there are bound to be things which interest them less. If your child feels like they don't have to love school, it'll be easier for them to talk honestly with you about their frustrations and difficulties. This will make it more straightforward for you to see where your child needs your empathy and encouragement the most.

> **Deputy Head (Quality of Education, Curriculum, Data):** *I think it's naive – and especially in sixth form colleges, where it's a totally different environment – to expect students to work all these things out for themselves. They can't just work out how to be independent and know the expectations if we haven't set them up in a clear way to begin with.*
>
> If you asked your child to tell you what is likely to be different in Y12, would their list match the list on p215–217? If not, what does this show you about how to support them?

Set out below are two sets of conversation samples that put these principles into practice: the first is built around ways you can initiate conversations with your child; the second focuses on how you could respond to things your child tells you.

If your child is reluctant to talk about school in general, you may find it useful to go back to the material in Chapter 4 on constructive conversations. This chapter explains why it can be difficult for a teenager to talk about school and why it can be particularly difficult for them to sustain a conversation when they are upset. There is further guidance there for how to create conversation structures that help keep dialogue open and constructive (see p84).

★ Initiating conversations with your child

Set out below are some conversation starters. After each one comes an analysis to highlight the steps in the conversation that may help your child reflect constructively on what has changed now they are in sixth form.

I'll repeat the caveat that accompanies all the conversation sequences in this book: they are suggestions only and it's very unlikely that a conversation would involve all these ingredients at once. They offer suggestions for ideas you could bring in, using a structure and pace which suits your child. If your child decides they've had enough, it's probably counterproductive to doggedly keep going with a conversation that your child is no longer engaged with.

What did you do in Physics today? Give me the headlines. How does this connect with other material?

This sort of specific question is much more useful than a more general *how was Physics today? What did you do* is a question that helps your child learn because it encourages them to re-engage with the key ideas from the lesson. It's a similar approach to the one I suggested for KS3 conversations, but the difference for a KS5 student is the interest in headlines: KS5 courses have much larger syllabuses, and this means that students sometimes feel lost in the detail. Encouraging your child to talk to you about the headlines will help them stay anchored around the core framework of the course. This makes it easier then to learn detail, because each unit of detail can be pinned to the area it relates to. This makes it much easier for the memory to file it away in a place that connects to and strengthens other knowledge.

Asking about connections – either within a subject or to anything else at all (for example, current affairs, something on TV, life in general) – helps your child learn to knit things together. Harder tasks at KS5 often involve the need to combine different things at the same time. GCSE does this far less. Conversations that help your child look for links between different types of material will help them develop this skill.

What study advice have you been given at school? Do you agree with it or not?

This encourages your child to think about how they study. Asking them whether they agree with what they're hearing at school encourages them to reflect on the advice more deeply, especially if you ask them to explain their reasons. It's also a conversation that helps you understand what your child finds useful or not, and this will offer you ideas to refer back to if there are times later on when your child feels at a loss.

It's also an opportunity to show that you take your child's opinions seriously and this will help them learn that their own opinions are worth investing in. This makes it easier for a teenager to learn to think for themselves; the more they practise thinking for themselves, the better they'll get at it.

Think about your lessons today – what interested you the least? What interested you more? Why was this?
If a young child comes home and tells their parents that they loved something they did at school, the parent is often delighted. This is a lovely and natural response, but – if your child is going to develop their own opinions and their own sense of self – it needs to be equally possible to talk about what they enjoy less.

If you're keen for your child to do well at school, it might seem strange to be asking about what interested them the least, but the important bit of the question is *why*. Hearing their reasons about what didn't fire them up will help your child be clearer about what does pull them in. Building a clear sense of what they are genuinely interested in will help them make better choices during KS5 about university courses or alternative options such as apprenticeships or gap years.

There's a further benefit, too: if dropping the subject isn't an option, your child is going to need to see it through, even if it now leaves them cold. It's much easier to keep working on something if there's room to release the frustrations along the way.

> **Y12 Student:** *There's the anger – you've never going to be asked any of this in your job, that's the annoying bit – it's all who can recall the stuff the best. That's what defines who does the best on exams.*
>
> It's natural for teenagers to feel angry about school sometimes; does your child find it straightforward to express this?

What's your time plan for this week? Is there anything you're going to change from last week? Is there anything I can do to support you in this?
This question keeps the importance of planning in view, but asking – rather than telling – your child demonstrates your respect for their opinions. Showing this respect makes it more likely that your child will think carefully about what they are doing.

Asking about whether they'd like to make changes also keeps another principle to the fore: flexibility. Reminding them that they may need to experiment in how they plan their week will help them feel better about the fact that they may not hit on the best plan first time around. Getting better at planning takes practice, and it's important for a teenager to remember that there's bound to be some trial and error involved.

★ Responding to things your child might say

A KS5 student may be less interested in discussing school than when they were younger, but there'll be times when they tell you things all the same. The examples below offer some ideas for how you could respond.

I only got 54%. It's all so hard.
If your child is feeling the jolt of much lower marks than they are used to, there are two priorities. The first is to make sure they remember that the marks are going to be different because the context is different. The second is to avoid the risk that they become demoralised and disengaged; central here is to make sure they notice the progress they are making and don't fixate on what they can't yet do (see further, p160).

Creating the space for their feelings is a helpful first step: *How are you feeling about this? Would you like to talk about it now or later?* It's sometimes helpful to remind them that the heat of the feeling will fade: *How do you think you'll feel about this tomorrow?*

When they're ready to discuss the specifics of the situation, you could ask questions that encourage them to think about the different context: *You're at the start of a new syllabus now – how do you think this affects things? Are marks likely to be higher or lower than at the end of Y11?*

Encouraging them to take a balanced perspective is always constructive. You can do this by asking them about what they've already achieved as well as what they still need to do: *Tell me about the 54% you got right. What does this tell you about what you know? What were the questions you were hoping would come up? Which bits did you feel better prepared for?*

If your child is worried about how to move forwards, encourage them to focus on a manageable next step: *Closing down on the other marks is going to take time – it's natural to take time to adjust to new expectations – so let's be patient and keep the focus on the next step. What's the best thing to do this evening?*

If they're exhausted and need time to decompress, it might be better to continue the conversation on a different day. *I was wondering how you're feeling about that test now? Would you like me to be a sounding board while you chat through your thoughts?* Don't be surprised if the answer is *no*: as children get older they ask for help less. But an offer still has value even if it gets turned down: it reminds your child that you're there for them, ready to support if they need it.

I've got to write an essay but I've never done one before. The teacher was really unclear and I don't know what I'm supposed to do.
In the early stages of sixth form courses, teachers are sometimes less prescriptive about how to complete a task. This is because it's good practice for students to experiment and think for themselves about how to do something. Some students find this difficult: underpinning this may be a mixture of a fear of experimentation and a frustration that they may get things wrong. It's worth creating space for this first: *What's the most annoying part of this situation for you? Is it the frustration that your effort might feel wasted if you write the essay and your teacher then tells you it's not right? Or is it something else?*

The second approach that can be helpful is to encourage them to think about the benefit of trying something even if it's not quite right. *It sounds like you're going to have to experiment and see what happens. If you try an approach and the mark is disappointing, what will you learn from the experience all the same?*

The third thing to try is to encourage them to set boundaries around their efforts and establish realistic expectations so that the task feels more manageable: *How long does the essay need to be and how much time do you have? What do you think is reasonably possible to achieve in that time?* It's often helpful for them to remember that a task like this is in the *have-a-go* category: this type of formative work in the early stages of a course is all about *getting it done* rather than *getting it all right* (see further, p103).

> **Y12 Student:** *Some GCSE questions were really basic but some needed something much more complicated and so it's very hard to work out what the examiner will actually want. I don't feel like I can trust my own judgement about how to answer.*
>
> Is this something that resonates with your child based on their own experience of GCSE? Now they're in Y12, do they still believe that they need to be told how to do something in advance or that they can't trust their own judgement about how to complete a task?

I'm never going to get all this work done.
If your child feels like they are drowning in their to-do list then there are two things that will help. The first is to remind them there are only so many hours in the day: they'll have to prioritise some things and deprioritise other things. This might feel less shiny than getting everything done, but it's a valuable life skill all the same. The best opening question, therefore, is to find out how much time they think they realistically have.

Then – after your child has worked out how much time they've got – you can help them prioritise. The questions on p180 may help them with this, as will the advice on p121 about working out which is the *better* rather than the *best* plan.

If you think your child is spending longer on work than seems manageable, encourage them to speak to their teachers. *Have they set you a time guide for how long to spend on this? Does it seem realistic? If not, would it be worth asking their advice on how to adapt the approach so that it takes less time?*

Holding onto Y11 habits

This chapter has focused on the need to let go of Y11 in order to thrive in Y12. There are some students, however, who manage to hold on to their

GCSE habits right through the sixth form. Ironically, the students who are most likely to do this are the ones right at the top of the class. If your child has a work rate and memory that makes it look like high 90% is still possible, it'll be tempting for them to chase it, and this will reinforce the GCSE impulse to do *everything* rather than *something* and to follow instructions as precisely as possible.

★ Y11 habits for high-attainment students

If your child is in this category, I'm not suggesting that high 90s are a bad thing or that they should deliberately slack off in the spirit of finding a new work rhythm. But I am suggesting that you encourage them to see the risk that – seemingly bizarrely – these high scores can impede their ability to develop the dispositions that will allow them to thrive in genuinely challenging contexts.

I'd recommend that you still talk with them about the concepts in this chapter because – if they are as high-achieving as their marks indicate and they are aiming for top-ranking universities – eventually they'll move on to something sufficiently difficult to make them experience all the shifts I've outlined above. If their *must-do-everything* GCSE habits have continued throughout KS5 as well, these habits will be twice as entrenched.

For the last 10 years, alongside my school teaching commitments, I've taught undergraduates at Cambridge. The biggest difficulty I see these undergraduates encounter has nothing to do with the complexity of whatever it is I'm explaining to them. The biggest difficulty tends to be the de-GCSE-ification of their educational habits. At university, they find that they've got to make choices about what to think and how to work. If they've been able to duck out of these at school by assuming they're going to find a way, somehow, to get *everything* done, the shift is harder to achieve.

Student: *You don't have to make a decision if you try to achieve it all. You haven't had to make a choice about where to draw the line. It's not immediately visible what the consequences will be if you draw a line – you don't know what you're risking – it's easier to just do everything to the max. If you do everything then you know that you can't be disappointed with yourself because you couldn't have done anything differently.*

Trying to do it all often feels safer, but what are the downsides? If a teenager doesn't practise making decisions about what to do and what not to do, what skills do they miss out on?

KEY IDEAS

- Y12 is a very different experience from the end of Y11; you can support your child by helping them think about how and why things are different.
- Adapting to the different expectations of Y12 will help your child feel more confident and engaged with their work.
- Your child may need your support in setting clear boundaries around when they will start and stop working.
- Your child may need you to listen and empathise when they're finding something difficult.
- You can support your child by providing the counterbalance that helps them keep schoolwork in perspective.
- Your child may want you to be less involved than when they were younger; this is a healthy sign of independence, but it's still reassuring for a child to hear you offer to support them, even if the offer gets turned down.

CHAPTER 12

Getting ready to leave school

Student: *You get talks about how these are A levels, these matter, these will get you into uni. It feels more high pressure.*

Does exam stress increase or decrease in the sixth form? When I was doing the interviews for this book, I got mixed answers. Some students said the process felt more familiar and this made it feel better; some students said the stakes were higher and this made it feel worse. As the Y13 exams get closer, sixth form can feel like a curious blend of *been here before* and *this time it's different*.

In this chapter, I'll be focusing on the aspects of the process that are specific to the sixth form. I'll be looking at the connection between sixth form and what happens next, offering guidance for how you can help your child make sensible decisions and maintain a balanced perspective about their next steps. At the end of the chapter, I'll look at the run-in to the final exams, highlighting guidance that you can reuse from previous chapters and explaining where it might need to be adapted to the Y13 context.

Some of the material in this chapter refers specifically to the transition to university. For many sixth-formers, this remains the most likely next step. The options available, however, have increased significantly over the last few years and university may not be the best choice. The careers guidance service at your child's school will have information about alternatives such as apprenticeships; I'm hoping that much of the advice in this chapter will still be useful even if your child is not going down the university route, especially the sections that relate to thinking about decisions in advance.

When does your child need to decide?

When should your child start thinking about what they'll do next? *Don't leave it too late* is the usual advice. *Get your UCAS form in early; if you're applying for a workplace training programme instead, don't do the application when you're hard up against the deadline.* The concern about *leaving things too late* means that some teenagers and their families feel that it's a good idea to have a plan in place sooner rather than later.

On the surface this seems sensible, but for teenagers, starting things earlier means starting things younger. When your child starts whatever comes next, they'll be 18 or 19. If they're thinking about post-school options when they are still only 16, will they have any idea of what is going to suit their 18-year-old self? As your child's experience of each subject develops, they'll have a much clearer idea of what types of course or programme they're likely to thrive on; if they try to decide this too soon it's like choosing a meal in a restaurant with only half a menu visible.

For the majority of Y12, if your child has very little idea about what they want to do next, this isn't a bad thing: it means they're remaining open-minded. The summer term of Y12 should be time enough to start thinking about post-school options in earnest: your child will know themselves better by then and they'll have a clearer idea of their strengths. If they're still finding it hard to decide by the start of Y13, it may be that they'd find it more constructive to take a gap year and make their decisions after their exam results are in.

In the context of exam stress, there's an additional downside to thinking ahead too soon. In the Introduction, I set out the idea that stress and investment go hand in hand: the harder you try at something, the greater the disappointment if it doesn't work out (see further, p11). As your child moves towards their final exams, their grades will be tied to some very specific consequences. The longer a plan has been in view, the greater the emotional investment can become and the greater the risk that your child feels that they *have* to get their grades. This increases the risk of problematic stress levels (see further, p116).

> **Deputy Head:** *There's all the fear of what the future looks like: they don't know enough about what it'll be like. They don't have the overview – all they've got is the jeopardy.*
>
> - What could you do to help your child feel less jeopardy about the future?
> - What could you do to help your child remember that there are multiple routes through life?

Discussing choices in advance

What counts as a good choice? Every time we give a piece of advice to a teenager, we end up shaping their perspective on what a good choice should look like. *Pick a subject that you love! Find something you're passionate about! Do what makes you happy! Make sure you're ready for a competitive application! Check out the rankings: how will future employers view your degree or qualifications?*

It's worth pausing to think about the messaging: does the advice make the choice more straightforward or more complicated? Does it create reasonable, balanced expectations about the future? Will it help your child maintain a resilient, flexible outlook or does it increase the pressure in a way that makes it harder for your child to maintain healthy, constructive work habits?

> **Student:** *Not having a dream is OK. Not everyone has a dream.*
>
> Does your child feel pressure to have their future mapped out? What is the upside to not having a fixed idea of what you'd like to achieve in life?

Let's explore in more detail now the messaging within different types of advice, unpicking the – sometimes unhelpful – implications that may sit in the shadows.

Pick a subject you love! Find something you're passionate about!
Surely there's nothing wrong with this one? I'm not so sure I'd agree: the concept of *loving* a subject or career path is attractive, but it's also a bit unrealistic. I think – as students go – I was fairly high up the scale of being interested in what I was studying. I worked hard and I chose to continue with the subject when I went into teaching. That's still quite a long way from *loving* it, though, and I've always liked to think that I'd have been interested in many other degrees in a similar way. Similarly, when it comes to careers, I'm a huge advocate of the value of being a teacher: it's a job that is meaningful, challenging, invigorating and worthwhile, but it's still a mixed bag, and some aspects of the job are more lovable than others.

The problem with the idea of *find something you're passionate about* is that it implies that if you're not passionate about it, then it's not the right choice. Interests change over time: are *love* and *passion* really necessary for a worthwhile way to spend the next few years? I don't think so: what's necessary is the belief that the programme will be worth the investment. The student needs to be motivated to keep doing the work. They need to feel there'll be a return on their efforts. If it brings joy, that's tremendous, but the more realistic threshold is for a teenager to hope that they will grow and develop as they do it.

Do something that makes you happy!
You can't be about to question this one too! Doesn't everyone want their child to be happy? I don't want to sound too much like a grinch here – like any parent, I really do want my children to be happy. But this advice runs the risk of falling into the category of a simplified generalisation (see further, Chapter 6). No one gets to be happy *all* the time.

Teenagers are still learning their expectations for adult life: the more realistic these are, the happier they'll be. Chasing an unrealistic dream rarely works out well. I'd agree 100% with the sentiment behind *do something that makes you happy*, so long as it's tempered with some healthy, balanced, realistic thinking. No degree option, training programme or job is entirely blissful. Wouldn't it be better for a teenager to hear this: *there'll be ups and downs whatever you choose; think about what feels like a good fit for your values and preferences, but remember that there'll still be some tough parts. Know this in advance and you'll find it easier to make your way through in a way that is optimistic, cheerful and resilient.*

> **Child and Adolescent Psychotherapist:** *'I just want you to be happy.'* How is a teenager supposed to be able to fulfil this? It's impossible. No one is happy all the time. Happiness is just a feeling that comes in and out.
>
> - Is your child using fulfillable metrics – such as the fit with their interests and strengths – for choosing what to do next, or are they looking for something less straightforwardly fulfillable, like happiness?

Make sure you're ready for a competitive application!
Is aspiration off the list too? No it's not: aspiration is a good thing. But I'd say that the aspired-for goal needs to be something which will be valuable to the individual child if they're going to find long-term worth in it. The challenge with this is that it can be difficult for a teenager to separate *valuable-because-others-approve-of-it* from *meaningfully-worthwhile-for-me*.

In Chapter 1, I discussed the idea of prestige bias and our natural impulse to copy the things that other people respect (see further, p28). *Valuable-because-others-approve-of-it* exerts a strong pull: I can still remember feeling a surprising internal resistance when I decided I didn't want to be a doctor. It felt strange to walk away from a career that had such wide approval.

There's no guarantee that the life choices which work for others will work for your child. A training contract at a prestigious law firm might be impressive but it's not a surefire pathway to future well-being. An accountancy apprenticeship or doing economics at a high-ranking university might receive general approval from others, but that doesn't mean it's the right option for a particular teenager. A job needs to pay the bills, of course, but if the only return it offers is a high salary then think about all the aspects of life that might end up in deficit. *If you didn't need the money, would you do the job for free?* If the answer is *no*, will the salary really be enough to make up for the cost on time and lost opportunities in other parts of their life? Would there be a different sort of job which offered a higher return when salary and job satisfaction were combined?

If your child's chosen pathway is highly competitive, they'll need to factor that into how they prepare, but it's worth double-checking that they've chosen this pathway for reasons that go beyond the fact that other people think it's impressive. If it's going to work out for them, they need to be clear about what it offers them, personally, and this should connect to their own values. They're much more likely to succeed at something if they feel it is worthwhile, and they are much, much more likely to feel motivated, energised and fulfilled.

Check out the rankings: how will future employers view your degree or qualification?
Actually, I'm not going to quibble with this one: it'd be problematic if it didn't feature to some extent in the decision-making process. But it's worth being alert to how limited the value of the answer is. If your child has a clear aspiration for a particular career, they need to know the standard steps which make up the pathway, but they also need to know

that success in this pathway depends upon more than just setting foot on the first step.

A high-ranking university or course carries a certain cachet but does it mean that someone is definitely more likely to get an individual, specific job as a result? Certainly not – think of all the other variables in the mix such as work experience, interview skills, the subjectivity of whoever is making the decision, and the tenacity needed to keep on making applications until something lands. Does a particular degree or qualification mean that your child is definitely more likely to succeed in the role if they do get the job? Again, clearly not.

Thinking about far-off outcomes has its place but it doesn't guarantee future success. This means that the benefit this question yields is limited. What's more, the question has a cost: it risks distracting attention away from something much more useful.

The much more answerable, useful question is something more specific. It's focused on the process, not the outcome: *Which parts of your skill set are your strengths? Which option is most likely to nurture those strengths while you are studying?* These questions focus the decision around developing skill sets in a way which enables your child to maximise their potential. It encourages them to think about and play to their strengths; this – more than anything – is going to be what helps them find a way to thrive as an adult.

★ Constructive questions about choices

Here's a set of different questions which will help your child think about the process. They encourage a teenager to have realistic expectations and think sensibly about which choices are likely to give them the best chance to fulfil their potential.

- *What are your strengths? Which parts of your skill set would you like to be stronger by the end of the next phase? Which options would facilitate this and why?*
- *How do you like to learn? Do you enjoy reading about things in books or would you rather be out there, learning on the job?*

- *Do you prefer something structured or do you like more freedom to plan your own work? If you're thinking about a university degree, what are the pros and cons of more – or fewer – contact hours?*
- *If you're keen to do a university degree, which of your school subjects do you find you choose to work on first? Why is that? What does this show you about what pulls you in and what you're less interested in?*
- *How do you feel about exams or coursework? Would you rather a degree course built on exams or would you rather be assessed on work that you do during the course?*
- *Are you looking for an experience that is similar or different to your experiences so far? What sort of surroundings would you like to live in? Big city or not? What's behind these preferences?*
- *What's likely to help you during the tougher parts? There are bound to be ups and downs: how do you feel about being nearer or further away from home?*

There is, of course, one more factor that will shape your child's thoughts about next steps. They've got to be realistically achievable, and that means there's got to be a good match between entry requirements and your child's predicted grades. I've encountered many families who go at this in a way which is cart before horse: they focus on the destination first, and then try to get the predicted grades to match. This is rarely a good idea, as the next section will explain.

Predicted grades

Predicted grades are all about expectations: if there's a mismatch between expectations and reality, this is unlikely to be helpful to your child (see further, Chapter 1).

If the predicted grades don't match your expectations – or your child's – and you're tempted to try to argue the case for something higher, please pause and think this through. *But they need a particular grade for their applications!* OK – those are the entry requirements for a particular course – but if your child is not already on track for these grades then the logic is all back to front. If your child sets their sights on a course which doesn't calibrate to the reality of where their work is today, this is not a good game plan. They should be thinking – realistically – about where their grades are likely to sit and choose a course which plays to their skill set. They'll thrive much better in a setting where the fit is right.

I can't think of any student I've known who's benefited from an inflated prediction. It sets a baseline that the teenager needs to pretend to be something they're not; this is no good for anyone and – if the inflated grade means they get an offer which they then struggle to meet – the risk increases that they'll feel problematically anxious about what results day will look like. This is likely to make it harder for them to do well. It's worth repeating the opening message from p10: **problematic levels of stress make it harder for a student to do well**.

But the offer will motivate them to work harder, runs the counter-argument. I've heard this many times over. For your child, you know the specifics; I'm dealing with generalities, but a sustained, raised work rate tends to need intrinsic motivation. This is why Chapter 5 focused on how to motivate your child by focusing on the process, not the outcome. It's tempting to believe that a university offer or similar will change the motivation landscape, but I'd encourage you first to unpick why their current output is as it is. There's a thin line between trying to initiate change and problematising a situation that might benefit instead from understanding and support.

Y13 Student: *People believing in you is positive but too much is too much. Too much belief that it'll be fine places a lot of expectation on you.*

- How might it feel to your child if you tell them you're certain that they can get higher grades?
- Will it be easier or harder for your child to be open with you about the pressure they feel?
- Will it be easier or harder for your child to be honest about what they are finding difficult?

The UCAS personal statement

This is a book about exam stress, not how to get a place at university. I'm including a section on the UCAS personal statement, though, because it's often something that teenagers find difficult. It can end up taking a disproportionate amount of their focus for weeks on end; this impacts how on top of things they feel during the summer term of Y12 and the autumn term of Y13, and – as will be a familiar refrain by now – teenagers tend to work better when they feel things are going well. If your child can move through their personal statement in a way that feels lighter, they will feel happier and the rest of their schoolwork will probably end up in better shape.

Is the personal statement their work?

My other reason for including a section on the personal statement is that parents often try to get involved. *How many people have you shown this to so far?* This is usually my opening question if a pupil shows me a draft. *Just my mum, and my dad, and they suggested my older brother should read it as well and I was thinking about showing it to my mum's friend because she did Maths and said she'd take a look. And I've shown it to my form tutor, of course, and my Maths teacher and I've got to send it to the Head of UCAS by Friday, but maybe you could read it first too?*

As a general rule, I'm all for feedback. It's usually useful – but not always. Too much feedback can make the process more complicated, more time-consuming, more stressful. In any case, your child's personal statement is supposed to be authentically theirs: push it through too many filters of other people's opinions and their voice may get lost. The personal statement should be your child's representation of themselves: write it for them – or edit it heavily – and inevitably you're overlaying it with your version of how you think your child should present themselves. Would this really – in the long run – be constructive? Would it help them end up on a course where they are likely to thrive, independently, on their own?

> **Student:** *In form groups, we started working on personal statements very lightly in February of Y12 and we were finished around late September in Y13. Our teachers really pushed it – our form tutors were checking up on us – we were looking at example personal statements in form time and commenting on them. There was a culture of people talking about how their personal statement was going – it was something that everyone was doing – so there was a lot of talking at break times and lunchtimes. I think there was definitely a lot of pressure – there was a sense of 'This is what a good personal statement looks like: if it's not that then it's not good.'*
>
> - Has your child started working on their personal statement? What are their thoughts about its importance?
> - Does your child think the personal statement is something that is straightforward or difficult to do well?

★ Supporting your child's personal statement

The personal statement serves two purposes: it's designed for universities as a selection tool but it's also a valuable opportunity for your child to crystallise a snapshot of who they are, what they've done and what they're hoping to be. There's plenty of guidance available through UCAS about what the different sections of the personal statement should contain. I'm not going to double up on this, but I am going to offer some thoughts about the process of writing one.

First, there's a tipping point where starting the personal statement earlier makes it harder. It's clearly not a good idea to start it the evening before the deadline, but if a teenager starts it too soon, they're simply not ready to write it. They're not far enough along in their sixth form courses; if they start writing it too early in Y12, they'll only need to rewrite it again later because their most valuable material probably won't come from their experiences in the first half of Y12. It's worth getting an outline of possible material in place by the end of Y12: this is so that there's time over the summer to fill in the gaps if there are gaping holes in the material, but the final drafting of the statement is best done as late as the school timeline allows. This is partly so that your child has the benefit of being further along in their subject knowledge, but also so that the personal statement does not distract for too long from the everyday process of moving forwards with schoolwork.

Second, as a parent, the best way to support your child is to enable them to write their personal statement authentically, for themselves. Here's a framework that may help you do this. The aim is to intervene as little as possible: if your child is looking for help, the best starting point may be to show them this section and see what they think.

- **Start with a list:** if your child has looked at examples of personal statements, they'll have been looking at a finished version, but the first step for the personal statement looks very different from the final outcome. The best starting point for a personal statement is usually a scrappy, messy, bullet-pointed list of what they've done or read, work that they've completed that exemplifies skills, areas of interest, the bits of the degree they think they're most interested in and so on. The guidance on the UCAS website provides a steer for the sort of content that might be needed.
- **Tidy up and take stock:** step two is for your child to tidy their list, sorting the bullet points into categories which help them see which material relates to which section of the statement. Sorting the list into categories will help your child see which material they're likely to cut and it'll show them if there's an area that's looking a bit scant. If they do their list just before the end of Y12, there's time over the summer to fill in the gaps in their material.
- **Sharpen it up:** then comes the process of sharpening it up: *essay on Shakespeare* is too vague. Much better is to be more precise, specifying title, key points and so on. If they've listed a podcast they've listened to, what did they learn from it? If they went to an exhibition, can they detail at least one thing they remember? What are they interested in and why? If the list starts to look like there's far too much content, that's fine – whittling it down can come later – the priority at this stage is for your child to see what's available.

- **Listen to them talk out loud:** step four is where – if your child wants this – parents can help by listening to their child's ideas. *Choose a few things from the list – any you like – and tell me more about them. Explain the idea to me as if I were five years old. Help me see why it's interesting.* One of the main blocks teenagers face in writing their statement is that they try to jump too quickly into language that sounds smooth or impressive. They don't spend enough time thinking, in language that is comfortable for them, about what it is that they really want to say. Talking the content through in familiar, easy language first will make it much easier to find the words when they start to write it down. It will also allow you as a parent to hear what your child is most interested in: their voice will change, they'll look different when they're talking in a way which is genuine. You can reflect this back to your child: *You really lit up when you told me about the civil rights movement. Tell me more about why you've found this so interesting.*

Overall, here's the key principle: try to step back from telling your child how to sound impressive; keep your focus on listening to the areas where they have most to say and where they are most willing to think further. If you do this, your child's ideas will develop in a way that is authentic. This will turn the personal statement into something that helps them develop their thoughts; you'll find that the end product is much better than if you'd artificially warped it into something that's yours, not theirs.

> **Student:** *I had friends who ended up saying they had read things when they hadn't. Starting the personal statement in Y12 can mean you feel you have to be somewhere when you're not there yet.*
>
> - Thinking about who you *should* be can turn into a distraction from noticing who you *are*: if, as a parent, you take an interest in your child's ideas, is this more or less likely to help them express these clearly?

Waiting for offers: Plan A and Plan B

Once applications have been made, your child will have to wait for offers – or rejections – to come in. This can take months. Waiting for offers can be a tense time: they come in at different rates and there are often surprises. Your child may have a preferred option from the outset, and there may be disappointments along the way. If your child is too focused on one option, the waiting will be harder and the disappointment may be more destabilising if things don't work out. As a parent, you can help your child through this process if you encourage them to maintain a balanced perspective.

★ Discussing the pros and cons of Plan A and Plan B

Once your child has worked out their preferences, it can be natural to start focusing on whatever the preferred post-school option is. But it's always helpful to have a Plan B in the background in case offers or grades don't arrive as hoped.

It's worth taking a deliberately balanced perspective on the options. It's natural to be more aware of the upsides to Plan A and the downsides to Plan B. Balancing things out means remembering the following two questions:

- What are the downsides to Plan A?
- What are the upsides to Plan B?

If your child much prefers the prospect of Plan A to Plan B, there's no point pretending they are equally desirable. Balancing things out doesn't mean pretending that everything's equally great; instead, it means keeping alternatives in mind so that your child stays flexible and adaptable (see further, Chapter 6, p122).

Conversations in advance also means that the words are there – already familiar – if they're needed on results day. The tears may still fall – that's natural while the disappointment is still raw – but if your child has kept thinking about the benefits of Plan B, they won't feel as lost as if they'd fixated only on why Plan A was worth trying for.

> **Y13 Student:** *What does help me is things of substance – so, for example, applying for uni – working through things of substance – if you get this grade then this is the option, if you get this other grade instead, then this is the option – this helps you see what the options are. Hearing what else is available and why it's still good – that's really helpful.*
>
> - What is your child's first choice likely to be? Why is this their first choice?
> - What would your child's Plan B look like? Have they thought about it as much as their Plan A? What does this show about the natural imbalance in how we think about options?

★ Getting those grades

Chapter 11 focused on the ways in which KS5 is different, educationally, from KS4. The process of sitting the exams, however, is remarkably similar. As a parent, it's really a re-run of the principles already outlined in Chapters 9 and 10; you may find it helpful to refer back to this material. If you want to help your child get their grades, it's largely about helping them maintain a healthy day-to-day rhythm, acting as a sounding board so that they can think through and feel more confident about their revision decisions, and keeping their spirits up by celebrating the small wins in the here and now.

The progression from KS4, however, is that usually the role for the parents reduces. Children are older and more independent. They are likely to need and want your input a bit less, but it still makes a big difference to know that it's available. *Would you like me to listen while you chat through your plans for the weekend?* The answer may be *no*, but that doesn't mean the question is pointless.

The other difference from KS4 is that the wish for it all to be over may be stronger. *Revise, turn up, write, repeat.* By the time your child sits their exams, this cycle will have looped round and round through KS3 assessments, GCSEs and all the practice assessments in KS5. It can be tempting to try to motivate your child by telling them *not to stop running until the race is over*, but focusing on one big finish line at the end makes the race very long, and – even at 18 – your child is still young enough for time to feel like it's passing frustratingly slowly.

It's helpful, therefore, to celebrate as many small finish lines as you can along the way. It will help your child feel like they're getting there and the moments of whooping will provide a welcome, restorative antidote to the ritual of opening the books *again*.

It also offers one further benefit: when your child does cross the line of their very last exam, the feelings can be more mixed than they're expecting. Finishing school is a huge leap into something very different: newness and loss are all intermixed. Celebrating the smaller finish lines will take the heat off the big one: the jolt of it actually, finally, really being over will be a bit easier to handle.

> **Student:** *What were the main differences between A levels and GCSEs? One of the weirdest things was how much more tiring it was. It would always surprise me how much more tiring it was even though it wasn't full days every day like GCSE.*
>
> Is your child more or less tired than they were at GCSE?
> How can you help your child maintain a rhythm that doesn't leave them too exhausted to work properly?

What has your child learned?

So, here we are: it's coming to an end. In the exam years, the school experience is inevitably imbalanced. Grades get the majority of the attention, but that's not all your child will take with them when they leave school.

One of the curious things about growing up is that it happens so incrementally that it's sometimes unnoticed. Think of the surprise that children often show when they revisit somewhere from their early childhood: *I can't believe it's all so small!* They know they've got bigger, of course, but it can take something external to make them really feel the difference between how they are now and what they were then.

This applies to all of the ways your child has grown up and developed, including the attributes that aren't as easily quantifiable as percentages in school exams. Let's leave the grades on one side for a moment. Which characteristics, values, skills or qualities has your child developed? I'm not going to give you a list – this question is for you and your child, not me. The point I need to make is that if these things aren't talked about, they won't be as visible to your child as the daily, unmissable reminder that currently, for Spanish, they're on 64%.

As your child approaches the end of school, there's value in giving them the opportunity to notice how much they have grown as a person. In those side-by-side moments of time, such as walking the dog or laying the table, when everything is so easy and familiar that there's comfortable room for a slightly bigger question, it's worth encouraging the thought processes that will help them see where they've got to. Doing this brings two benefits: it will help your child feel settled in their sense of self, but it will also remind them that the value of their time at school isn't measured in grades alone.

Asking questions is often a bit better than just commenting on what you see. *That was so kind of you – I'm so proud of you for saying that to your sister*: there's a role for direct praise like this, of course there is, but it does the work for your child. So there's additional value in encouraging your child to see it in themselves, for themselves.

★ Noticing what they've learned

The list of your child's most important characteristics will be personal to you and to them. What's below is just a sample of the sorts of questions that exemplify how you could help your child notice characteristics in themselves. I've built it around four attributes which I happen to believe are important – adaptability, positivity, honesty and compassion – but the list is subjective and you could adapt the questions to suit other things.

You'll notice that many of the questions are anchored to situations which are pre-sixth form. This is because it's often easiest for teenagers to think openly about things which are comfortably far off in the past. I'm not suggesting you ask the questions all at once, though; dropping the occasional question in here and there will help your child learn to notice and value the things that aren't grades.

Adaptability
- *Can you remember what it was like at the start of Y7? What advice would you give to your younger self now? What does this show you about what you've learned on the way?*
- *Which bits of KS4 took you by surprise? Why is it difficult to predict what something will be like in advance?*
- *What do you think might be different for you next year? If it's not as you expect it to be, what can you remember that will help you adjust?*

Positivity
- *What has helped you stay cheerful in the past?*
- *What do you think were the hard bits of KS3? Did they offer you anything useful even though they were difficult? What do you know now that you didn't know then?*
- *Part of positivity is remembering that disappointment fades over time. Do you agree with this? Can you remember something that felt really important in Y10 but which you feel differently about now?*

Honesty
- *Which types of honesty need the most courage?*
- *It's easier to be honest with some people than with others: what do you think you've learned about how to listen to others if you'd like them to be honest with you?*
- *What advice would you give to your younger self about fronting up to problems?*

Compassion
- *How does it feel when you've got something wrong? Can you think of a time back in primary school when you felt like this? What would you say to your younger self now to help them feel better?*

- *What have you learned about how to help others feel better? Why is it harder sometimes to give yourself the same advice?*
- *Is it possible to avoid making mistakes altogether? Why do you think this is? Is it straightforward to remember this – compassionately – when you've made a mistake?*
- *What do you think you'll tell yourself going forwards to help you find the confidence to see past the mistake and focus on what you can do next?*

The last day of school

Do you remember the words from the very first page of this book? *I don't want to talk about it – you don't understand – leave me alone – why can't you just **go away**?*

Let's imagine that you're now at the end of the process. It's the last day of school. You've helped your child make it through: your compassionate interest in their day-to-day experiences has helped them make sense of the often confusing world of adolescence. Your readiness to listen respectfully to their opinions has helped them learn how to think for themselves and how to respect the opinions of others. Your willingness to ask questions has helped them balance out their perspective. Your common-sense focus on maintaining a healthy rhythm has given them the energy to make it right through to the finish line, strengthened rather than reduced by the race.

Let's imagine you're sitting in the kitchen with your child: they're happy to sit there and have a chat, they're open to sharing what makes them feel proud and they can be honest and brave about seeing what they learned from the things they got wrong. Can you imagine yourself telling them this? *I hope that results day will allow you to feel that you've wrapped all of this up with a bow. But don't forget that grades are really just that: they are wrapping paper. They are nowhere near as important as what's there underneath. Sitting here, listening to all that you've told me, I am so proud of who you've become.*

Good luck for the journey: from one parent to another, I'm cheering you on.

> **Student:** *I think the best advice is to know that it's not set in stone, you can change things.*

KEY IDEAS

- Exams can feel more significant in Y13 because exam grades are the pathway to university courses or training programmes. To balance out this pressure, you can help by encouraging your child to stay open-minded about alternative options.
- Some teenagers aren't ready to decide what they'll do after school when they're at the start or middle of Y12; they'll find this decision easier as they get older and clearer about the person they'll be when they leave school.
- Your child will make better choices if they think about what motivates them and which of their strengths they are keen to develop.
- It is rarely in a child's interests for a school to inflate their predicted grades.
- You can help your child if you encourage them to use their personal statement as a way to develop their own ideas; it is not a good idea to write your child's personal statement for them.
- Finishing school is a time for you and your child to reflect on and celebrate all that they've learned so far and the person they've become.

Acknowledgements

So many thanks are owed to so many people. Thank you to my family for supporting me while I wrote this book; thank you to my husband for believing in the book; thank you to my teenage sons for their upfront feedback about how the book – and indeed my parenting – could be better. Thank you to all the school and university students who I've taught over the years. Thank you for your openness: you have been courageous and strong in ways you probably didn't realise at the time. Thank you to the teachers whom I've worked with and talked with: we've celebrated together about our students' best moments and we've shared the sadness of seeing the enormously difficult situations that some young people find themselves in through no fault of their own.

Thank you to all the people who have been directly involved in this book. Thank you to all the teachers, mental health professionals, support staff and students who agreed to be interviewed. I promised you anonymity so I can't name you here, but I'm so grateful for your help with this project. Thank you, too, to Marina Gardiner Legge, Kathryn Faulkner, Dan Silverman, Michelle Holder, Angela Cheetham, Alison Thomas, Rahim Hirji, Ellie Marsh, Helen Carey, Alice Byram, Katie Martin and to Holly Jarrald, Sarah Skipper and the team at Bloomsbury. You have all helped this book to move past its ragged first draft into the shape it is now. Thank you.

Bibliography

Works directly referred to in the text are listed in bold below.

Atkinson, C., Brown, K.-A. and Soares, D. (2019), 'What can schools do about examination and test anxiety'. Available at: https://ofqual.blog.gov.uk/2019/03/15/what-can-schools-do-about-examination-and-test-anxiety/.

BBC Bitesize (2023), 'How to deal with exam stress in the run-up to GCSEs and Nationals'. Available at: www.bbc.co.uk/bitesize/articles/z8dw239.

Biddle, L., Gunnell, D., Sharp, D. and Donovan, J.L., 'Factors influencing help seeking in mentally distressed young adults: a cross-sectional survey', *British Journal of General Practice*, 54(501), 2004, pp248–253.

Blakemore, S.-J., *Inventing Ourselves: The Secret Life of the Teenage Brain* (London: Penguin Random House, 2018).

Brown, B., *Atlas of the Heart: Mapping Meaningful Connection and the Language of Human Experience* (London: Vermilion, 2021).

Carver, C.S. and Scheier, M.F., 'Engagement, disengagement, coping and catastrophe', in A.J. Elliot and C.S. Dweck (eds.), *Handbook of Competence and Motivation* (New York: Guildford Publications, 2005), pp527–547.

Cassady, J.C., *Anxiety in Schools: The Causes, Consequences, and Solutions for Academic Anxieties* (New York: Peter Lang Inc. International Academic Publishers, 2009).

Childline (2019), *Childline Annual Review 2018/2019*. Available at: https://learning.nspcc.org.uk/research-resources/childline-annual-review#heading-top.

Childline (2023), 'How to deal with exam stress'. Available at: https://www.childline.org.uk/info-advice/school-college-and-work/school-college/exam-stress/.

Children's Commissioner (2024), *Children's Mental Health Services 2022–2023*. Available at: https://assets.childrenscommissioner.gov.uk/wpuploads/2024/03/Childrens-mental-health- services-22-23_CCo-final-report.pdf.

Csikszentmihalyi, M., *Beyond boredom and anxiety* (San Francisco: Jossey-Bass Publishers, 1975).

Culler, R.E., and Holohan, C.J., 'Test anxiety and academic performance: The effects of study-related behaviours', *Journal of Educational Psychology*, 72(1), 1980, pp16–26.

Davis, H.A., DiStefano, C. and Schutz, P.A., 'Identifying patterns of appraising tests in first-year college students: Implications for anxiety and emotion regulation during test taking', *Journal of Educational Psychology*, 100(4), 2008, pp942–960.

DfE (2019), *Achievement of 15-year-olds in England: PISA 2018 Results Executive Summary*. Available at: https://assets.publishing.service.gov.uk/media/5f20292e8fa8f57ac3af2d11/PISA_2018_England_Exec_summary.pdf.

A.J. Elliot and C.S. Dweck (eds.), *Handbook of Competence and Motivation* (New York: Guildford Publications, 2005).

Family Lives (2023), 'Exam stress'. Available at: www.familylives.org.uk/advice/teenagers/school-learning/exam-stress/.

Gladwell, M., *Outliers: The Story of Success* (London: Penguin Random House, 2009).

Haidt, J., *The Anxious Generation* (London: Allen Lane, 2024).

Hembree, R., 'Correlates, causes, effects, and treatment of test anxiety', *Review of Educational Research*, 58(1), 1988, pp47–77.

Howard, E. (2020), *A review of the literature concerning anxiety for educational assessments*. Available at: www.gov.uk/government/publications/a-review-of-the-literature-on-anxiety-for-educational-assessments.

Huberty, T.J. and Dick, A.C., 'Performance and test anxiety', in Bear, G. and Minke, K. (eds.), *Children's needs* (3rd edn). (Bethesda, MD: National Association of School Psychologists, 2006), pp281–291.

Kahneman, D., *Thinking, Fast and Slow* (London: Penguin Random House, 2012).

Mental Health Foundation (2018), '60% of young people unable to cope due to pressure to succeed'. Available at: www.mentalhealth.org.uk/about-us/news/60-young-people-unable-cope-due-pressure-succeed.

Mind (2023), '14 ways to beat exam stress'. Available at: www.mind.org.uk/information-support/your-stories/14-ways-to-beat-exam-stress/

Morgan, N., *The Teenage Guide to Life Online* (London: Walker Books, 2018).

Morgan, N., *Blame my Brain: The Amazing Teenage Brain Revealed* (London: Walker Books, 2022).

Murphy, L. (2022), *Not working: Exploring changing trends in youth worklessness in the UK, from the 1990s to the Covid-19 pandemic*. Resolution Foundation. Available at: www.resolutionfoundation.org/app/uploads/2022/06/Not-working.pdf

Music, G., *Nurturing Natures: Attachment and Children's Emotional, Sociocultural and Brain Development* (Abingdon: Routledge, 2024).

National Health Services England (2018), *Mental Health of Children and Young People in England, 2017*. Available at: https://digital.nhs.uk/data-and-information/publications/statistical/mental-health-of-children-and-young-people-in-england/2017/2017.

National Health Services England (2022), *The Mental Health of Children and Young People in England, 2022*. Available at: https://digital.nhs.uk/data-and-information/publications/statistical/mental-health-of-children-and-young-people-in-england/2022-follow-up-to-the-2017-survey.

National Health Services England (2023), 'Help your child beat exam stress'. Available at: www.nhs.uk/conditions/stress-anxiety-depression/coping-with-exam-stress/.

OECD, *PISA 2015 Results (Volume III): Students' Well-Being* (Paris: OECD Publishing, 2017).

OECD, *PISA 2018 Results (Volume III): What School Life Means for Students' Lives* (Paris: OECD Publishing, 2019a).

OECD, *PISA 2018 Insights and Interpretations* (Paris: OECD Publishing, 2019b).

OECD, *PISA 2022 Insights and Interpretations* (Paris: OECD Publishing, 2023a).

OECD, *PISA 2022 Results (Volume I): The State of Learning and Equity in Education.* (Paris: OECD Publishing, 2023b).

OECD, *The PISA Happy Life Dashboard: Visualising Key Indicators on Student Well-being from the PISA Survey* (Paris: OECD Publishing, 2024).

Ofqual (2025), 'Coping with exam pressure: a guide for students'. Available at: www.gov.uk/government/publications/coping-with-exam-pressure-a-guide-for-students/coping-with-exam-pressure-a-guide-for-students.

Public Health England (2016), *The mental health of children and young people in England.* Available at: https://assets.publishing.service.gov.uk/media/5a80c3e240f0b62305b8d06c/Mental_health_of_children_in_England.pdf.

Richerson, P.J. and Boyd, R., ***Not by genes alone: How culture transformed human evolution*** **(Chicago: University of Chicago Press, 2004).**

Rickwood, D., Deane, F.P., Wilson, C.J. and Ciarrochi, J., 'Young people's help-seeking for mental health problems', *Australian e-journal for the Advancement of Mental Health*, 4(3), 2005, pp218–251.

Ricky, E., *Ideas in Psychoanalysis: Anxiety* (Cambridge: Icon Books, 2000).

Rosenshine, B., *Principles of Instruction* (London: International Academy of Education, 2010).

Salaheddin, K. and Mason, B., 'Identifying barriers to mental health help-seeking among young adults in the UK: a cross-sectional survey', *British Journal of General Practice*, 66 (651), 2016, pp686–692.

Schuler, P.A., 'Perfectionism in the gifted adolescent', *Journal of Secondary Gifted Education*, 11(4), 2000, pp183–196.

Sharfran, R., Egan, S. and Tracey, W., *Overcoming Perfectionism: A self-help guide using scientifically supported cognitive behavioural techniques* (2nd edn). (London: Robinson, 2018).

Sherrington, T., *Rosenshine's Principles in Action* (Woodbridge: John Catt Educational Ltd, 2019).

Siegel, D.J., ***Brainstorm: The Power and Purpose of the Teenage Brain*** **(London: Scribe, reprinted 2021).**

Smith, Dr J., *Why has nobody told me this before?* (London: Penguin Michael Joseph, 2022).

Spielberger, C.D., *Manual for the State-Trait Anxiety Inventory for Children* (Palo Alto, CA: Consulting Psychologists Press, 1973).

Student Minds (2024), 'Exam Stress'. Available at: www.studentminds.org.uk/examstress.html.

Taleb, N., *The Black Swan: The Impact of the Highly Improbable* (London: Penguin Random House, 2010).

Taleb, N., *Antifragile: Things that Gain from Disorder* (London: Penguin Random House, 2012).

Wright, S., *Exam Nation: Why our obsession with grades fails everyone and a better way to think about school* **(London: Penguin Random House, 2024).**

Index

A levels 61, 63
    see also KS5; university/training course applications
adolescent development 26, 29, 51, 62, 76–7, 112, 132, 149–50, 210, 214, 242–4
anger and frustration 73–5
anxiety and stress 9, 36–7, 67, 73, 91, 97, 117, 180, 214, 234
    see also exam stress
artificial intelligence (AI), AI 93–4
associative memory 44–6

behavioural problems 176
boredom and repetition, schoolwork 61–2
brain function, human 44–6, 76, 112, 132, 210
burden of praise 31

career plans 33–6
catastrophising 161, 164
complexity and rigidity, exam content 63
compulsive behaviour 183
conformist bias 28–9, 41
conversations about school, creating constructive 72, 130
    advice misinterpreted as criticism 79–80
    anxiety about making a problem bigger 80, 85
    asking exploratory questions 82–3
    counterproductive responses 85–9
    creating space for emotions 74–5, 92
    difficulties in verbally expressing emotions 76–7
    difficulty asking for help 79
    downside of asking 'How was your day?' 131–2
    guidance for helpful responses 89–91
    KS3 pupils 130–5, 152–5
    listening properly 75, 77–8, 81–4, 92
    offering solutions 77–8, 82, 83, 85, 92
    response considerations 84–5
    talk and energy levels 131
    timing a talk 131
    useful questions to ask 132–4

why conversations can be difficult 73–4
conversations about sixth form
    helpful responses to your child 221–3
    initiating 218–21
conversations with the school, constructive 144–5
cost:benefit ratio 106–8
criticism 32, 79–80, 85, 87–8, 92, 153
    see also conversations about school, creating constructive

decision-making and revision/homework 115–16, 121–2, 188–9, 190–1
demoralised, grades and feeling 36–40
disappointment, balancing out 160
disengagement, pupil 12, 64, 94, 95–6, 175–7, 188

eating disorders 9, 183
emotions
    creating space for 74–5, 92, 221
    experiencing new 51, 56
    validation of 75, 108–9
    verbally expressing 76–7
empathy 38, 84, 107, 109
energy levels, pupil 62, 67, 69, 131, 147, 156
engagement strategies, pupil/child 60–1, 63, 106–7
evaluative thinking 120–1
evolutionary behavioural theory 28
exam stress
    commonality of 9
    impact on performance 10–11
    incorrect assumptions about 11–13
    parental influence 10, 14, 16–17
    see also well-being concerns, serious
exam technique 61, 63
experience of school and exams, parents' 13, 43, 46–8, 56
exploratory questions, asking 82–3
extracurricular commitments 66, 179

failure, fear of 11–12, 96
feelings see emotions
financial investment in education 49

flexible attitude to outcomes, need for a 33–40, 41, 97–8, 123–4, 171–2, 186
funding, school   59
future goals/aspirations   33–6

GCSEs
   connection to KS3   150–1
   length of syllabus coverage   48, 61, 63, 64, 69
   mark criteria   61, 63
   pass rates   38
   subject choice   164–6
   transition from Y11 to Y12   208–9, 224
   see also exam stress; grades/results
'getting ahead,' issue of   138–9
grades/results
   blurring 'want' and 'need'   116–17
   demoralisation   36–40
   flexible attitude to outcomes   33–40, 41, 97–8, 123–4, 171–2, 186
   KS3 level   129–30, 146–57
      targeted follow-up strategies for different %   157–60
   results day   124–5
   schools' success   58–64
   sixth form   216, 221–2, 224, 233
   uncertainty about   25–6, 33–4

health issues, physical   183–4
help, difficulty of asking for   79
hierarchy, pressure of   149–50
higher education *see* university/training course applications
homework   93–5
   clear start times and finish lines   101, 110, 179
   cost:benefit ratio/incentives   106–8
   getting it done *vs* getting it right   103–6, 110, 181
   giving space to offload   109, 110
   improving engagement   106–7, 181
   over-promising   182
   planning and organisation   100–1, 180–2
   problem with to-do lists   178–9
   reducing time   108
   sixth form   214, 222–3, 225
   teacher guidance   103, 110, 181–2
   time commitments   66–7
   timetabling   102–3, 178–9
   use of tech and AI   93–4

work rhythm during KS4   178–82
   see also motivation and work habits
hyper-engagement   12–13, 94–5, 106, 108, 164, 188

incentivising your child   106–8, 204–5
independence, developing   82, 156–7, 210–11, 215, 225
inspections and accountability, school   58–9
internet/online access   136
   see also social media

Kahneman, Daniel   44, 112
KS3   48–9, 64, 101, 102
   checklist questions   136–7
   exams/tests   129–30, 142, 143–4, 146, 147, 148–51
      being realistic about mistakes   163–4
      dealing positively with disappointing results   155–7, 158–60, 167
      parental guidance for when a result is 59% or below   158–60
      parental guidance for when a result is 60-85%   160–1
      parental guidance for when a result is 85% or above   162
      talking about   152–5, 167
   GCSE subject choice   164–6
   issue of 'getting ahead'   138–9, 147
   managing your child's smartphone   135–6, 147
   opening conversations about school   130–4
   pressure of hierarchy in school   149–50, 167
   responding to problems   140–2, 144–5, 147
   unrealistic expectations - child and parent   143–4
   working with the school   144–5, 147, 159–60
KS4   48–9, 64
   disengagement: creating a counterbalance   174–7
   effective work rhythms/homework   178–82, 186
   the end of Y11   202–5
   establishing a balanced perspective   173–4, 186
   extra tuition   198–202, 206

focusing on things beyond GCSE - life skills etc.   174–5, 186
serious well-being concerns   182–5, 186
thinking about expectations   169–71, 186
widening the margin of tolerance   171–2, 186
see also revision
KS5
compared to KS4   207–12, 224
finishing school   244–5
healthy study routines   214
helping your child adapt   213–18
constructive conversations   218–23
new learning processes   215–16
personal growth/development   243–4
Y11 study habits   207–9, 224
see also university/training course applications

labelling children, adults   27–8
levels of achievement, differences in   33–4, 36–8, 39–40, 41
listening to your child   75, 77–8, 81–3, 92

mark schemes   49, 61, 63, 69
marketisation of schools   58–9
memories of exams, parents'   13
mental health issues   183–4
mistakes, making   98–9, 104–6, 163–4, 173
motivation and work habits   94–5
disengagement   95–6
fear of making mistakes   98–9
importance of results and motivation   97–8
over-emphasis on plans and organisation   100–1
over-work and hyper-engagement   99–100
reinforcing the need to do better   96–7

neurodiversity   19–20

offloading frustration   108–9
overworking *see* hyper-engagement

parental expectations for KS4   169–72
parental influence on exam stress   14, 16–17
pass/fail mode   115, 120
peer pressure   29

perfectionism   13, 164
personal growth/development   242–4
personal statements, UCAS   235–8
perspective comparison, teenager and adult school   42, 49–50
differing experiences of time   50, 56
experience of emotions   51, 56
experience of self   51, 56
identifying adult assumptions   46–8
understanding differing values   52–3, 54–5, 56
understanding school today   43, 48–9, 56
perspective for KS4, establishing a balanced   173–4
disengagement: creating a counterbalance   175–7
focusing on things beyond GCSEs - life skills etc.   174–5
perspective on exams, changing
blurring 'want' and 'need'   116–17, 121
building a balanced perspective   118
choosing between two options   121–2, 126
decision-making and revision/ homework   115–16, 121–2
nuanced thinking *vs* soundbites   118–19, 126
pass/fail mode   115, 120
preparing for results day   124–5
scoring thoughts out of ten/evaluative thinking   120–1, 126
self-blame   113–14, 120
unhelpful simplified thoughts   111–17, 126
'what-if?' questions   117, 122–3, 126
see also grades/results, exam; KS3
Plan B   123, 173, 239–40
plans and organisation, over-emphasis on   100–1
praise   31–3, 41, 244
pressure on teenagers today   15
prestige bias   28, 29–30
procrastination   12, 96, 178–9, 188

quick-response cognitive processes   44–6, 112

relaxation   71, 131, 136, 147, 180
repetition of syllabus content   61–2, 64
resilience   106, 120, 135
results day   124–5
revision   180

decision-making/prioritising   115–16, 121–2, 188–9, 190–1, 206
extra tutoring   198–202
familiarisation *vs* memorisation   190
helping a worried child   192
hyper-engagement   188
input to output learning   189–90
outcome and self-blame   114, 120
pass/fail thinking mode   115, 120
planning   187–9
procrastination and disengagement   188
question of 'enough' revision   193–7
resources and methods   188, 189–90
see also homework
rewards and treats   32, 106–8, 204–5

screen time boundaries   68, 180
secondary school today   48–9, 57–8, 128–9
   complexity of environment   132–3, 147
   inspections and accountability   58–9
   strategies for raising grades   60–1, 69
   impact on students   61–4
self, a child's sense of   26, 27, 51, 56, 163
   adults labelling children   27–8
   copying others at school   28–9, 41
   praise   31–2
   sibling influence   30–1
serious well-being concerns   182–3
siblings, influence of   30
simple thought patterns, adolescent   111–17, 126, 161–2
sixth form *see* KS5; university/training course applications
smartphones, managing   135–6, 147, 179, 183
   see also social media
social media   15, 67–8, 69, 136
solutions, offering   77–8, 82, 83, 92, 203
strengths, finding your child's   39, 40, 41, 161

stress *see* anxiety and stress; exam stress
syllabus start times, earlier GCSE   61, 63, 64, 69

teacher guidance   103, 110, 181–2, 193
technique, exam   60–1, 63
time, adult and child experiences of   50, 56
time pressure
   extracurricular commitments   66
   homework   66–7
   is your child too busy?   65–6
   social media   15, 67–8, 69, 136
to-do lists, problem with   178–9
tolerance, widening the margin of *see* flexible attitude to outcomes, need for a
tutoring, extra   198–202, 206

UCAS personal statements   235–8, 245
uncertainty, stress of   25–6, 33–4
university/training course applications
   discussing subject choices   228–33, 245
   predicted grades and university applications   233–4, 245
   rankings   231–2
   UCAS personal statement   235–8, 245
   waiting for offers: Plan A and Plan B   239–40, 245
   when to think about   227–8, 245
unrealistic expectations   143–4

values, understanding differing   52–3, 54–5, 56

'want' and 'need,' blurring   116–17, 121
well-being concerns, serious   182–5
'what if?' questions   117, 122–3
work ethic *see* motivation and work habits

Y11: keeping going   202–3
   incentivising the final push   204–5
   ways to help your child   203–4

Praise for *The Parent's Guide to Exam Stress*

'Katharine Radice has serious credentials in the world of education and is attuned to the everyday concerns of parents. She expertly and considerately guides parents in how to support their children and young people, walking us through different approaches in a way which considers the important impact of the parent-child relationship and how each child is individual. How I wish I'd had this book during my own children's exams!' **Dr Sheila Redfern, consultant clinical child and adolescent psychologist and author of** *Reflective Parenting* **and** *How Do You Hug a Cactus?*

'A book that sets out to challenge many of the assumptions and fears that parents hold about a critical period in their children's lives - but one that does so with care for the reader. Written beautifully and, at its heart, very wise.' **Sam Wallace, journalist for the** *Daily Telegraph*

'I wish I'd read this book before we went through exam hell with our teens - it's steeped in practical knowledge that helps you support your kids to try their best and be happy with the results.' **Katie Martin, columnist for the** *Financial Times*

'Clear, sensible and invaluable.' **Henry Marsh, author of** *Do No Harm*

'This impressively comprehensive book is one to begin as soon as your child starts secondary school and to keep coming back to. It offers new insights, clear explanations and strategies which are firmly practical and positive. It will help parents help their child grow stronger and more resilient through the storms of tests and exams.' **Nicola Morgan, The Teenage Brain Woman and author of** *Blame My Brain*

'A must-read for parents. Speaks for the child with an adult's insight and a teacher's understanding.' **David Walker, Executive Director, BSA Group**

'Katharine is a go-to expert - this guide is a must for parents who want to understand more and help.' **Michael Senior, founder NetSixthForm network for UK sixth form leaders**

'This guide is full of practical, supportive and kind advice, designed to keep the channels of communication open. If your child is facing exams, read this guide - it will make such a difference to the journey.' **Marina Gardiner Legge, Head of Oxford High School & Vice President of Girls School Association 24-25**

'Thoughtful, practical advice for Y7-13.' **Sir Jon Coles, CEO United Learning**

'This book is filled with humanity and realism. The particular range of Katharine Radice's experience is unrivalled and she offers perspectives which would benefit every parent of a school-age child.' **Gareth Mann, Master of the King's Scholars, Westminster School**

'What a great book! Honest, thoughtfully challenging and exactly what is needed for students and the adults in their lives. Full of practical tips, well-explained tools and relevant to all students.' **Dr Alice Byram MD, President of the Digital Health Section at the Royal Society of Medicine, Founder of TwinVita**

'Sensitive and astute; authoritative and informed by experience and authentic case studies. This book creates a practical, non-judgemental relationship with the reader.' **Kieran Earley – former CEO and Principal, The British School in the Netherlands**

'This readable and no nonsense book will help anyone understand and develop the right strategy for their child, developing resilience that will help them in these exam years and beyond.' **Professor Guy Williams, Downing College Senior Tutor, Cambridge**

'Sensitive and thought-provoking: this book will help parents balance ambition with wellbeing.' **Andy Johnson, Head, Truro School**

'This is a book I will be going back to again and again while my children are in school. Katharine Radice's experience of working in schools and as a parent shines through - you feel guided by someone who really cares and understands. I will be recommending this book to all my friends with children in secondary school. It's well organised and easy to find the information you need and full of really helpful and practical advice.' **Dr Joana Taylor Tavares, British Psychology Society Chartered Psychologist**

'A reassuring, evidence-based guide to helping young people navigate the challenges of exams.' **Tim Lomas, Vice Principal, Hills Road Sixth Form College**

'Wise and worthwhile. Katharine's extensive experience as an educator and a parent makes this book a useful companion for parents.' **Simon Detre, Senior Deputy Head, The Beacon School; ISI Inspector**

'Katharine not only deepens a parent's understanding of the pressures their child faces but also offers thoughtful and practical advice on how they can support them.' **Jaime Lythgoe, Head of Upper School, Royal Grammar School Guildford**

'What sets this book apart is the quality of its advice: practical, balanced and rooted in a genuine understanding of both academic rigour and adolescent development.' **Michelle Holder, Deputy Head (Pastoral), The Godolphin and Latymer School**

'An excellent book, full of accessible and practical advice for parents.' **Michael McKenzie, Headteacher, Alexandra Park School**